ITALIAN GREYHOUNDS
TODAY

ANNETTE OLIVER

RINGPRESS

ACKNOWLEDGEMENTS

My grateful thanks to all who sent photographs and other material from all over the world. Appreciation must also go to the late Mrs M. B. Garrish for her constant support in my efforts to record the history of the breed.

Published by Ringpress Books Ltd,
PO Box 8, Lydney, Glos, GL15 4YN

First Published 1993
© 1993 ANNETTE OLIVER
This edition published 2001

ISBN 0 948955 92 9

Printed and bound in Singapore
by Kyodo Printing Co

CONTENTS

Ch. Philtre Fayetta Of Dairylane: 1972-1983.
(Philtre Fanado – Philtre Snaffles Storytime).
Toy Group winner, Crufts CC and Reserve CC.

Pearce.

Purchased at eight weeks from Mrs Rae Lewis, 'Fay' was a very special person in the Dairylane household as well as in the ring. She was the foundation of those that followed and will always have a special place in my heart.

Chapter One

ORIGINS OF THE BREED

The exact origin of the Italian Greyhound is not easy to trace, although there is a lot of evidence to support the theory that Egypt was their first home, in common with various other hounds. Wall murals, monuments, tapestries and other artifacts of an early period all indicate the existence of these small hounds. Historian Alexandro Glugi wrote that "there are many breeds of dog whose shape and disposition developed into the characteristics of each breed. ...There are, however, characteristics common to all breeds and the climate and environment must have played a part in the development of the various breeds." Certainly, the little Italian Greyhound would have appreciated the warmth of the shores of Egypt.

The Marchesa Maria Luisa Incontri Lotteringhi della Stufa (Del Calcione Italian Greyhounds in Italy) who died in 1991, was a well respected authority on the breed and she carried out a great deal of research into its origins. She believed that it was likely that the Italian Greyhound was a breed in its own right, not dwarfed from the Greyhound, and that it had originally come from Egypt and then spread to Greece and Italy. The expansion of the Roman Empire is of great significance, because as the armies travelled they were accompanied by their canine companions, together with the rest of their entourage. The popularity of Italian Greyhounds during the Early Renaissance (1400-1500) is indisputable as they appear in so many works of art during that period. Claims for the Italian Greyhound can also be made in literature. *The Canterbury Tales* by Chaucer (late 14th Century) contains the following lines in the verse about the Prioress....

"And she had several small houndes
She would be feeding
With roasted flesh, or milk, or fine white bread
And bitterly she wept if one were dead
Or someone took a stick and made it smart ....."

A reference is made to several of the hound family of dogs in an extract attributed to Dame Juliana Berners in *The Boke St Albans*, which was written in the fifteenth century:

"Headed like a snake
Neckeyed like a drake
Footed like a catte
Tyled like a rate
Syded like a team
And chyned like a bream"

During the eighteenth and nineteenth centuries the north Mediterranean region had a large proportion of small greyhound-type canines, while in the South the common dog was similar in type, but often with longer, coarser hair, more like a jackal. British homes tended to keep the variously coated small terriers. Written evidence confirms that one of the Italian Greyhound's greatest supporters in Britain, Mrs B. F. Scarlett (1854-1934), firmly believed that Italy was the first home of the breed, dwarfed gradually from the large greyhound of Africa. Mrs Scarlett was adopted by her father's sister and her husband, Sir Percy Florence Shelley, when she was a baby, after the death of her mother, and as a result she spent a great deal of her youth in Italy travelling in her uncle's yacht. As a teenager, she recalls seeing many ownerless Italian Greyhounds scavenging in Italy.

THE FASHIONABLE IG

The exact time in history when the Italian Greyhound became fashionable is difficult to place, but there is no denying that the breed was a great favourite in the Royal Households at the time of the Stuarts (early 17th century) and other European court circles. Looking at paintings of this era, it seems that some of these dogs were of the larger type. Confusion with the Whippet often arises but it is generally believed by canine historians that the Italian Greyhound was crossed with the small terriers, so readily available, particularly in the North of England, for the purpose of providing small, tough, running dogs for rabbiting and racing, and this dog later became known as the Whippet. The original crosses were not always suitable but when these were crossed again, the smaller Whippet resulted. Some Whippets also resulted from crossing with the ordinary Greyhound and various other varieties, but evidently in 1899 Rawdon B. Lee, author of an absorbing book on the dogs of the day, firmly believed that the Whippet was still known in many localities as an Italian Greyhound, which, he says, it could not have been because it was not pure bred.

Whatever the truth of the matter of origin, the Italian Greyhound was a great favourite in the nineteenth century in Britain and Italy. In the USA Italian Greyhounds appeared in the first annual New York Benched Show of Dogs, under the auspices of the Westminster Kennel Club, at Gilmour's Garden on May 8th, 9th and 10th 1877. In class No. 42 for Italian Greyhounds (dogs or bitches) Madam Annie Tille of 214 West 47th Street, New York, had two exhibits: 'Nannie', a light fawn, aged four years, won first prize, plus ten dollars, and 'Lillie', a fawn with a white neck, nine months of age, won second prize and three dollars. The other exhibits in the class were Mr L. N. Meyer's Daisy and three pups, a fawn, ten years, full pedigree, and C. Bellany Culver's Bonfanti, a cream, aged six years and four months.

In Britain at this time many large houses boasted several Italian Greyhounds. The master of the house very often had large hounds, such as Greyhounds, for hunting, and the lady of the house would keep Italian Greyhounds as companion dogs. This does not mean that all IGs were kept this way; some certainly led more adventurous lives, hunting in the forest. In a number of Renaissance paintings the dogs often seem to have white on them, or in some cases they appear all-white, but in the nineteenth century the solid fawn Italian became the most desirable. It is not clear why this happened. Signora Incontri wondered if the albino colouring featured in the early paintings was 'poetic licence' and in reality the dogs were varying shades of fawn – but this is something we shall never know.

Much more to the detriment of the breed was the fashionable craze at this time for smaller and smaller specimens. The result was skinny and frail, shivery creatures, with apple heads. These failed to appeal to the majority, and the general pet-owning public soon became enamoured with other more fancy breeds. The Pekingese was one that particularly caught their imagination and it quickly usurped the place of the beautiful Italian. These days it is hard to imagine a tiny Italian weighing something like 4lbs (less than 2 kg); this is Chihuahua size to us in the twentieth century. Then, as now, it behoves us all to breed to the requirements of the Breed Standard or Scale of Points or whatever other system is in use. It is not for owners, breeders, exhibitors of any era to change the dog to suit a whim of fashion.

A writer of the time said "mere mites some of them were, not more than 4lbs or 5lbs weight, with legs thinner than the shank of a Broseley straw pipe, skull round or apple-headed and a mouth or jaw very much overshot." Amusing as this sounds today, it could have been the end of the Italian Greyhound as we know it, and what an awful shame that would have been. To miss out on the joy of owning one of these delightful dogs hardly bears contemplation.

FORMATION OF IG BREED CLUB

This then was the sad state of affairs when the British Italian Greyhound Breed Club was first formed in 1900 with Mrs Bessie Scarlett at the helm as Secretary and with much support from a number of eminent fanciers of the period. The English Kennel Club had been formed in 1873 and the American Kennel Club was formed slightly later, in 1884. In my opinion, it was the advent of exhibiting dogs that saved the breed in the end. The keen exhibitors and owners in the UK, in the USA and elsewhere in Europe set about defining Standards for all the dog breeds. In other words, a set of points and a detailed description was drawn up so that breeders could aim towards producing fit and healthy animals with the typical 'look' required for the breed.

IGS IN THE SHOW RING

In Britain, Miss Henrietta Mackenzie, later known as Mrs H. M. Shearer, was the keenest of exhibitors, winning a great many prizes with her dogs. She was a professional singer and had a passion for the music of Handel. Her involvement with the breed began in 1867. Mrs Scarlett kept a great many personal records, and she wrote: "Miss Mackenzie's strain are the only strain that breed clear peach fawn. Without any red tinge and some with a good deal of white. Very pure colour. Mostly small, not over 8lbs." It is recorded in a dog paper of 1900 that Miss Mackenzie received a visit from the Rajah Venugopala Bahadur of Madras. He required two Italians to go back to India with him, and he picked out a bitch and dog pup, which Miss Mackenzie promised to ship out "when old enough to ship and bear the journey without risk".

Many of the aristocracy became involved in the new sport of exhibiting dogs, and fortunately for us, some took an interest in the club that had been formed. Many titled ladies and gentlemen owned Italian Greyhounds and left invaluable records of their dogs in their diaries. The

Miss Mackenzie's
Juno. 1894.

Mrs B.F. Scarlett, c. 1875.

Mrs Cottrell-Dormer (Rousham) at home with her dogs, c. 1900.

Marchioness of Waterford, Lord Abinger and his mother Lady Abinger (related to Mrs Scarlett), Mrs Cottrell-Dormer, Sir Musgrave Horton Brisco and his wife, Baroness Campbell Von Laurentz, all helped to stimulate interest in the breed at the shows. Mrs Scarlett was a talented artist and wrote detailed accounts of the Italian Greyhounds of her day. Concerning her own dogs, she wrote in 1868: "Percy bought me a most beautiful thoroughbred Italian Greyhound puppy aged five months, colour dusky fawn – its mama belonged to Victor Hugo – and so did it when Percy bought it. Mab was born on the Island (Guernsey), poor Vispo is dreadfully jealous of it and will not speak to Percy if it looks at him – or he at it – poor Vispo!" (Percy is,of course, Sir Percy F. Shelley, already referred to).

The cross-breeding with regard to the Whippet, although deemed necessary by some, was not without its problems. According to Miss Mackenzie's records it became extremely difficult to find an outcross from her own dogs that did not contain some terrier in it. Even when this was fairly remote it could result in puppies being born that were black and tan in colour. Manchester Terriers and English Toy Terriers were commonly mixed with the Italian Greyhounds, hence this colour combination. Ear carriage was also a problem, as often the puppies had the erect ear carriage of their terrier forebears instead of the rose ear of the Italian Greyhound.

Quarantine was not in existence at this time, and therefore several owners brought dogs back with them from holidays abroad. During the period when the 'Grand Tour' was the fashion and families spent the long and cold winters in Europe, several Italian Greyhounds found their way back to Britain and were incorporated in the breeding plans of the people that owned them. Again we are indebted to the detailed records kept by Mrs Scarlett, who so carefully noted the good and bad points of many of the dogs. The following extract is reproduced exactly as written:

"The Revd ... kept a few Italian Greyhounds belonging to his mother who died very old in 1904. One big one was his 'Tinker', a dark slate colour of quite 11lbs, if not over. On his mother's death, he offered Helen, Lady Abinger, two of them, as he had let his house and wanted to part with all but Tinker. So she and I went down there to fetch the two away – I asked him about the origin. The first dog was a dark slate and was bought in 1873 in Paris. The person who bought it was most particular to have one marked correctly of that breed – namely a few white hairs on the chest, called a 'jabot', four feet tipped with white, and half white hind feet. The French people considered these special good points in their breed. In 1875 they had their first pups and for twenty years they bred only for their own, never any admitted from outside, and then appeared a fawn, and since then they sometimes had a fawn. There was not a suspicion of black and tan about any of them and they were all clear colour, whatever it was. If any tendency to any other colours than black or slate, only pure-white and this is like the old dogs in old pictures."

Not everyone loved the breed. The Marchioness of Waterford's diary made it quite plain that her husband did not share her passion for Italians. Others were very protective towards their dogs – Sir Percy Shelley sacked the scene painter at his private theatre in Boscombe because he painted the dog's ribs with luminous paint and made them look like skeletons.

THE MACKENZIE IGS

The history of the Italian Greyhound is full of interesting anecdotes, and there is one particularly delightful tale, written in Mrs Scarlett's own hand, concerning a dog belonging to Miss Mackenzie that figured largely in the breeding of her dogs:

"This is the history of Jack, the foundation of Miss Mackenzie's breed – as she told me August

15th 1902.

"One Friday evening a pretty little well-bred looking dog was seen running about Smithfield Market, evidently lost, by the butchers whose market it is and who are always about. One of them, Charlie Covell by name, picked it up, another bought it off him for five shillings and soon after having it, another man also a butcher, offered him ten shillings for it, as it would just suit a cousin of his at Hornsey, who was looking out for a pet, but as he could not take it then, asked Charlie to keep it for him till Monday and then bring it to him at the market Monday morning.

"Covell assented to this, but was puzzled what to do with the dog, as he was in lodgings and could not take it there, so talking it over with a mate, the latter said 'Ask Miss Mackenzie to keep it till Monday for you, she's a doggy woman.' (Miss Mackenzie then lived close to the market with her brother and managed his house for him; he had a business as butcher's clothier there.) So off the dog was taken to Miss M who at once agreed to keep him till Monday, and found 'Jack', as he was called for a name, a very well bred, good little affectionate dog.

"On Monday morning, Miss M (knowing the rough side of the butchers pretty well) told their foreman to take the dog to the market and hand it over to Covell and not lose sight of the dog first in case they said it had not been delivered to her etc. Her foreman took the dog and found Covell in dispute with his would-be purchaser, who now said he would not give more than five shillings for the dog. Covell said he had offered ten shillings and so they began a regular row and a good many got into the matter and knives came out. One said 'I would rather cut the dog's head off than take only five shillings' and sure enough such things were only too likely to happen, when a 'butcher's row' is on, and knives are handy – they would have the dog's head off in no time!

"The dog got dismally frightened and the foreman seeing the dog's life was in imminent danger whipped out half a sovereign quick, put it down, saying 'Well, I'll give you ten shillings for him and take him back to the Missus' and off with the dog back again, quick as he could. On getting to the shop, he loosed the dog, who rushed into the back shop on to Miss M, threw his head over her shoulder, and gave such a sigh that she thought the dog would burst and must be very ill. Then the story came out. Miss M declared the dog knew all that was going on, and knew how near he was to being killed, and I think it quite likely. Miss M had the dog fourteen years after that before he died and he was four years then; he lived to the great age of eighteen years.

"His origin came out in a very curious way. She was showing Juno, one of his pups, at Birmingham, some two and a half years after Jack's death. Juno had won first and all she could, and she went to the refreshment room with her in her arms to get her some milk, when a young man said to her 'You've got a nice dog there' and asked her what her pedigree was. Miss M said that she had bred her. The young man kept on looking at the dog very hard and said 'Who was her father, what was his pedigree?'

Miss M said the dog was hers and had been bought in Smithfield Market, but she had no idea of his pedigree. The young man got very excited and said 'It is the dog! It must be the dog!' Miss M began to be frightened, thinking the dog must have been stolen. Then enquiries were made 'Was the dog alive? Could he see it?' 'No – the dog had died about two and a half years before.' 'What day of the week had he been bought, was it on a Friday night?' 'Yes', in such and such a month and year.

"Then the man said he was a jockey, his name Charles Burton; his father lived on the estate of an old gentleman near Cannock, Rugby, of great wealth and until he went into trainee stables he lived there with his father. The old gentleman (name forgotten) was eccentric and very rich and had imported two Italian Greyhounds he was very fond of. The pair had been imported by him from Italy. The bitch died but the dog was his constant companion. He went nowhere without it; even to the opera the dog went with him. He came to London and in the season was going to give a ball, and one of his fads was rather to get things himself and 'see about all sorts of concerns'. He wanted sweetbreads for this ball, and somehow got it into his head to go to the market himself for them.

"So off he set in his carriage with coachman and groom and his precious dog with him but on getting to the market and seeing the rough people about there, he saw he had made a mistake in coming there personally and at any rate the dog was best in the carriage, so he left it there, but the door was not properly fastened; the dog must have got uneasy at being left, and got out, slipped down, and so lost; when he returned the dog was gone. He was dreadfully grieved, bills went out and large rewards given but not until after the dog had been picked up and disposed of. Miss M did not see the papers regularly and never saw it. Was too busy with a lot of workmen to attend to and feed at all hours – the old gentleman never recovered from the dog's loss and was never the same again. He had died some years before. The dog was four years when lost and from particulars given, was certainly Jack."

It is interesting to note that others from entirely different civilisations were equally attracted to the Italian Greyhound at this time. About the year 1899 newspapers reported that Lobengula, Monarch of Matabele, saw an Italian Greyhound in Johannesburg and was determined to purchase the little dog. The dog's owner, Mr Luscombe Searelle, at first would not part with him, but the King was so persuasive that finally a bargain was struck. The exchange was for two hundred head of cattle – the value at the time being extremely high. It seems that the two Chiefs who were charged with the responsibility of transporting the little Italian Greyhound to its new master were told their lives would be forfeit if harm befell him, but sadly they came to grief in a battle, and there is no record of the fate of the dog.

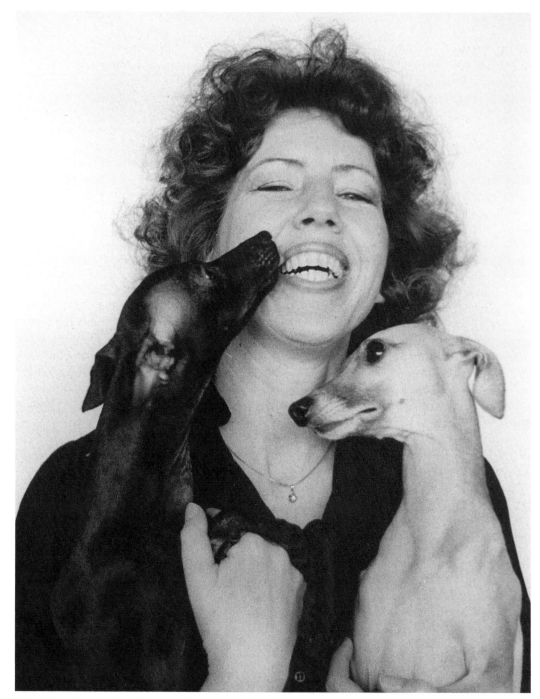

Birthe Bjorch with her Italians, Bianca and Vindhauses Giovana.

Chapter Two

THE COMPANION ITALIAN GREYHOUND

There are many things that attract lovers of Italian Greyhounds to the breed. Initially it must be the dog's graceful and flowing lines which are so pleasing to the eye. The range of lovely colours in the breed are all equally attractive and complement the beautiful shape. The Italian Greyhound may be any solid colour: fawn, blue, black or white; it may be one of these colours with white trim, known as 'Irish marked', or it may be pied, i.e. white with large patches of colour. Brindle is the only colour that is not allowed, nor tan markings on any of the blue or black dogs, as will be explained later. The shades of fawn are quite varied, from a bright golden fawn to a more blue-tinged colour, or as bright as red mahogany. The blue can also vary from a very dark blue to an almost grey type of colour. The shiny black-coated Italians are also very smart. To see an Italian Greyhound, Le Petit Levrier Italien, Italiaanse Windhondjes, Il Piccolo Levriero Italiano, to give just some of its names, either just standing or running free, takes the breath away. Add to this the delightful character of the breed, and you have the magical combination that is the Italian Greyhound.

This intelligent and fun-loving little dog is an ideal companion from the point of view of size. It is not so large as to present difficulties in terms of accommodation, feeding bills or when travelling, yet it is large enough to look a 'real' dog, with the added bonus that it is small enough to pick up easily. The breed has a fine velvet-like coat; it does not leave hairs all over the furniture, like some breeds, and there are no doggy odours either. All the Italian – or IG as it is often called – requires is a bed of its own, the use of the best chairs, and a regular (even daily) change of soft blankets. Of course, if you only own one IG as a pet, and in some cases even if more than one lives with you, you will soon discover that their favourite place to slumber is your own bed. If you cannot find your IG during the day, check the bedroom first – that is my advice!

Italian Greyhounds love to cover themselves up completely, without any help being required from their owners, and visitors are always amused to see a blanket move and realise there is little creature underneath. Blankets are picked up in the mouth and tossed and turned about, with the feet assisting in the task, until the blanket, or their owner's jumper that may have been carelessly discarded on a chair, disguises them completely. I have to add that they will do this on the warmest of days too, and sometimes you wonder how they can bear the heat. Sometimes they

Ch. Philtre Little Caesar in characteristic 'Italian' pose with front legs crossed. Owned by the late Mrs M. C. Fraser. Bred by Mrs R. Lewis.

will emerge panting, have a stretch, perhaps a drink and a look-about, and then recommence the procedure.

All Italian Greyhounds love to sunbathe when the weather is kind, and they appreciate a piece of matting or blanket on the ground where they may lie. It is advisable not to let them over-do the sunbathing as they really do get sunburn. The white and pale coloured ones will go really bright red and the fawns often turn quite black underneath. All owners should limit their dogs' exposure in extreme temperatures. In the house an IG will follow the sunshine around a room, placing themselves wherever they can feel the sun's rays best. Keep a check on this, however, as it can easily mean the dog perching on the back of a chair, or similar.

When you are considering owning any breed, it is important to take into account the commitments of the family members. If there are a number of small children, will the little Italian receive enough attention from its adult owners or will it just be a plaything for the younger element? On the whole, Italian Greyhounds like children, but it has to be remembered that these dogs are small and lively themselves, and sometimes the combination can be unwise. Will the children understand that the IG should not be brushed aside when it intrudes into the games and frolics of the youngsters?

An Italian Greyhound can easily come to harm if it is misguidedly pushed from a chair or surprised into leaping out of the way. This may not be a problem with larger and tougher breeds, but the long, fine-boned legs of the IG must always be borne in mind, and a bad landing can mean a fracture. This does not just apply when there are small children in the home. It is equally applicable if the prospective owner has a very busy coming-and-going sort of household, where an IG could easily become a problem. Access to staircases is best avoided when the Italian is a puppy.

EXERCISE
Exercise is a very flexible affair. If you wish to walk for miles, then the IG will oblige. If, on the other hand, your requirements are rather more sedentary, then the little hound will be content with the use of your garden and the run of the house. Sufficient fresh air to establish good health

Italian Greyhounds get on particularly well with their own kind. Myroak Maggi at Jemalsheva with her brood. Owned by Helen Davis.

is all that is necessary. Many older people find the IG very suitable from this aspect, as the need to exercise a larger pet can be too much for them, yet they have no wish to deny themselves the close and loving companionship that only a dog can give. An IG will let the owner dictate the most appropriate exercise routine.

In inclement weather, a small coat, preferably specifically shaped for an Italian can be worn. However, I do not think it is wise to wrap a dog in a coat all the time, as fresh air is the best tonic in the world. Italians absolutely hate wind and rain, as they feel every spot of rain and every gust of wind, so an owner should not expect them to participate in outdoor activities in these conditions. Snow is a different matter, and an IG will be happy to play in these conditions, but do not allow its enthusiasm or your enjoyment in watching its antics make you forget the time. An IG loses body heat very quickly, and while you may be considered a spoilsport for ending the fun, it is better to be safe than sorry.

The other essential ingredient for a walk or an outing is a 'hound shape' collar and a suitable lead, i.e. a collar that is wider at the neck where it is placed under the throat so that no undue pressure is placed upon the dog's delicate skin. A name disc should always be worn, with the owner's address and telephone number, in case some misadventure should cause dog and owner to be separated. Tatoo and microchip identification schemes are readily available.

GROOMING
As already stated, clean bedding is an essential, and it is the provision of this, combined with sensible good food and the essential minerals, that will keep an Italian looking good. As far as grooming is concerned, an occasional brisk rub over with a silky cloth or piece of velvet is all that is required. Bathing, to be done when necessary, is a simple affair with an IG. Any gentle shampoo is suitable, plus a large, warm towel to dry the dog. A hair-dryer can be used, but this should never be held too close to the dog's body for fear of burning the delicate skin.

BREED CHARACTERISTICS
A couple of Italian Greyhounds living together can be very amusing to watch, and sometimes, of

course, they can be infuriating! They will nuzzle in a bed together, often washing and licking and making sure the other is clean, but this often entails actually sucking each other's ears. This particular habit is as old as the breed itself; in the Vatican and in the British Museum there are sculptures of two IGs doing just this, and these are of Roman origin. IGs are most enthusiastic in greeting visitors and will bare their teeth in a grin; this smile can appear at any time and without any obvious reason. One of my own older dogs will often stir out of his warm bed at some point during the evening, and jump on my knee and just grin at me, as if assuring us both of our mutual admiration!

The long legs of an Italian are wonderfully flexible, and an IG's most characteristic pose when lying down is with the front legs crossed in front of it or bent under the body – an enchanting picture. However, an Italian Greyhound can often surprise its owner by the way it can leap up into their arms without apparent warning. It just seems to spring in the air like a Jack in the Box. You should always discourage a dog from jumping on to worktops in the kitchen, for safety reasons: the possible dangers from hot surfaces or sharp instruments are obvious.

There is, however, no cure for this habit of leaping up, and some do it more than others. I'm afraid you just have to learn to catch them, and after a while it becomes second nature! Never try to stop a dog in mid-flight by scolding, as the sudden sound of your voice – particularly if you sound cross – may affect the dog's judgement and landing. In the same way, if you enter a room and find your IG perched on a high and unsuitable surface, do not rush at the dog to grab it. Far from protecting the dog, this may result in it leaping haphazardly and injuring itself in the process.

Although I may have indicated the need for the IG to have its own dog bed, do not be misled into assuming this small dog will expect to sit sedately in this all the while. I am afraid more usually they expect to take over the most comfortable chair in the room, although they will be willing to share this comfort with their adored owner.

Perhaps I should add at this juncture that one is always owned by an Italian Greyhound, not the other way around! My own household currently contains two Whippets, three elderly Chihuahuas and a Pug living with my two veteran IGs, and all three breeds live together in harmony. However, introductions should be made with care when dogs are of different size and stature. IGs usually get on particularly well with their own kind, and with other breeds in the home, but the combinations must be chosen sensibly.

Canine companions that are too big and boisterous, or those that are small and excitable, will have to be supervised initially. It is rare for an IG take exception to another. If others visit the home or another is purchased, or indeed at dog shows, they will in the main lie quite happily together. A family of IGs that live together will always pile into one bed, no matter how many have been carefully provided by their loving owner. If one member of the group is feeling rather anti-social towards an incoming member, the approaching IG will usually get into the bed backwards in a submissive manner. It has frequently been reported that when an IG is unable to receive titbits or something special on offer, perhaps because it is ill or incapacitated, one of its 'family' will take back an offering to it.

Most IGs are not great barkers. If other breeds are kept which do bark it can encourage the IG, but in general they are not a yappy breed. They can 'sing' or howl, and certain sounds can increase this tendency. Many owners have commented how a certain piece of music or an icecream wagon horn, for example, has produced a vocal reaction. I must confess to owning a very lovable little fawn dog, who is particularly 'vocal' if we humans are at the meal table. Try

Tudor's Twiga makes some unusual friends. She is pictured with a hand-reared leopard (who is on a chain leash) and a redbuck at the William Holden Wildlife Education Foundation on the slopes of Mount Kenya.

S. Pinkus

as I might, I have not yet found a way of stopping this unless I shut him into his cage. My husband tells me it is because he is thoroughly spoilt and that I would not tolerate similar behaviour from any of our other dogs. However, I know that this dog's son, who lives with another family, does just the same thing!

FEEDING

As far as feeding is concerned, two smaller meals per day are preferable to one large amount. Most of the hound-type breeds find excessive quantities of food difficult to digest. A rest should always be encouraged after meals to aid digestion. Whatever the diet, fresh water must be available at all times; more will be consumed if an 'all-in-one' complete diet is used. Never give your IG pork or ham bones; these will cause severe stomach disorder. It is not advisable to give bones of any sort when the dog is left unsupervised. Flat rib beef or lamb knuckle bones are enjoyed; they help to loosen puppy teeth and they keep adult teeth clean. Cooked bones, however, will splinter and therefore their consumption should always be monitored by the owner.

Pet shops supply good hide chewy toys, which all dogs enjoy. In my opinion, the thin pencil-shaped ones are too risky, as they could get stuck in the roof of the mouth or be swallowed. Toy balls should not be so small as to be a risk by getting stuck in the jaws. I recently heard of a puppy of another breed that died after playing with a cat's toy ball; the ball had holes in it and the puppy's tongue got stuck causing a vacuum, resulting in the puppy's death. A sombre tale, I know, but it serves as a warning to all of us when we are choosing toys for our pets.

Another common trait amongst the hound-type dogs – and Italian Greyhounds are no different to the rest – is their total disregard for ownership. Never expect to tell an Italian to 'leave', as you can with some of the other breeds, and expect to have your dinner remain on the table untouched while you vacate the room. The Fagin character in Charles Dickens' story of *Oliver Twist* could have done no better than employ an IG or two in his gang!

HOUSE TRAINING

Some owners seem to find Italian Greyhounds difficult to house train. Whether it is the fault of the breed or their owners, I have no way of knowing, but I cannot say that I have found them any more difficult than any other breed. All dogs are individuals and so are their owners. Much depends upon the way dogs are housed, and the amount of time for training that is available from their owners. I would suggest that the best method is to try and take a young puppy outside on to a grass or paved area as often as possible in order for it to do what is required.

If you have purchased a puppy at about ten weeks or so, then you will probably be using a crate to house the youngster during the night and when you are out of the house and the puppy is left alone. In this case you should have a bed at one end of the crate and newspaper covering the rest of the area. Puppies are not in the habit of soiling their own beds, and from birth onwards a puppy will get up and move away from its sleeping compartment. If you have the litter yourself, all the same rules apply, but more times over if you are training several together. All puppies learn from their older companions, whether it be the dam or another IG that you own.

House training is a very time consuming exercise, but it is time so well spent. Whenever the puppy has had a sleep, or if it has been playing for fifteen minutes or so, it is worth taking it outside to the toilet area. If the puppy is only used to going on grass this can be a nuisance, particularly with bitch puppies who will be less than co-operative if requested to use paved areas, particularly at shows, when they are older. So it is therefore wise to try and use paved areas, as most will oblige on grass even if not trained to it, whereas the reverse does not necessarily apply.

From the beginning of this part of the Italian's education it is useful to have certain words used regularly as commands. It does not really matter what you say, but it is important that you always use the same phrase, as with any training exercise. If you keep repeating your command at the relevant times the puppy will soon connect the words with the action. This is invaluable when you want it to oblige at a certain time, such as when you are putting the puppy out last thing at night or when you are at a show. Routine with dogs is as important as it is with children.

If you allow a youngster to have complete freedom of the house then I think you are far more likely to have toilet training problems. Until you are reasonably sure that your young Italian is reliable, it is better to confine its activities to the kitchen or utility room, perhaps bringing it into other living rooms for short periods of play while you are with them. Newspaper can still be placed on carpets where they are playing, so that if any sudden tendency to bob down should be noticed they can be quickly put on to the paper.

During the day you must watch your puppy, and as soon as it gives any indication that it needs to go outside, you must let it out immediately. The puppy may go the door, it may suddenly leave what it is doing and rush to another part of the area, or it may go around in circles a few times. If you watch your puppy you will soon get to learn the signs! In the kitchen (or whichever room the puppy is housed in) place a sheet of newspaper on the floor in front of the door, so that if you are not around to open the door it will hopefully get the idea to use the paper. Always allow for the fact that nature must take its course shortly after a meal, particularly when with youngsters they are eating several meals a day.

Owners with male Italians will have to be extra vigilant if bitches are kept, particularly when a bitch is coming into oestrus or is actually on heat. All dogs will be eager to mark out territory at this time. Bitches also urinate more often at the time of the heat when they are most attractive to the males. Do not let them use the same toilet area, if possible. Exercise out on the street at this time also has to be curbed, or the neighbouring hounds will soon make their presence felt at your door. It is quite simple with a little IG bitch to carry her for a distance and then allow her to walk in a secluded area, or take her out in the car and then let her exercise.

No hard and fast rules can be given as regards house training, except that you must be patient and be prepared to work at getting your IG clean as young and as quickly as possible. If your dogs are to be a pleasure to live with, then this part of their social training is of paramount importance. The onus is definitely on the owner to be as vigilant as possible; praise like fury when the puppy obliges, and scold when it does not. It is no use smacking your puppy or getting upset. All puppies have to learn, and all owners have to be prepared for occasional mistakes. I feel all breeders should commence this training, even if they will not ultimately keep all the puppies in a litter, because then a new owner can carry on the work.

Chapter Three

CHOOSING A PUPPY

"What should I look for when I choose a puppy?" This is a question I have been asked on numerous occasions by prospective purchasers. If you are considering purchasing a puppy to exhibit, it is likely that the breeder will already have had first pick of the litter. However, this does not mean that you will not be able to buy a very nice puppy. In most cases the breeder will get as much pleasure from seeing a good specimen from their kennel doing well in the ring as from exhibiting it themselves. Many owners have been fortunate and have purchased a puppy that has become a Champion. This is more particularly the case when the new owner has only one IG, and both dog and handler benefit from a special one-to-one relationship. In this situation an owner can sometimes get more out of a dog – even if it is not the pick of the litter. The plainer puppy may blossom and perhaps turn into a swan after all.

The only certain way of having a total choice is when you breed your own litter and then you can watch the puppies every day from birth onwards. Those who do not require an Italian Greyhound for exhibition purposes will still wish to purchase a typical specimen of the breed, and while some of the factors considered to be a 'fault' in the show ring may not be of consequence to this type of purchaser, they still want to know what is aimed for in producing a show standard dog.

The advice I give to all to those enquiring about buying an Italian Greyhound is 'be patient!' Go to several shows and watch the breed being exhibited. Do not just look at the dogs that win on that day, but look at how they are bred, i.e. who is the sire and who is the dam? Find out about the parents' size, dentition and temperament – for every dog you see is the product of a pedigree. Try and work out the the type of Italian Greyhound that appeals to you in both looks and temperament – one that you would feel proud to own – win or lose. If, after visiting several shows and hopefully seeing some IGs in a home environment, you are convinced that this is the breed for you, the next step is to choose which kennel or line you want to purchase from.

HOUSING
Incidentally, I use the word 'kennel' to imply a breeder of IGs, as many Italian Greyhound breeders are not happy about their stock living in outside accommodation, believing that an IG

should be kept as a house pet. This can pose a problem for the serious breeder/exhibitor as inevitably numbers mount up. One solution is to allocate a separate room to use for sleeping quarters, for rearing puppies, and as a safe, comfortable place to accommodate the dogs when there is a houseful of visitors.

In some instances outside buildings or exercise runs have been designed to accommodate the IGs, and providing the accommodation has all the creature comforts that an IG expects, these dogs can be perfectly comfortable. However, I must stress that above all, this breeds need human companionship; they cannot thrive as 'kennel dogs'. If you have to resort to this type of home for an IG, each dog must be given its own time in the house too. Never forget they are all individuals.

On a personal note, I have always kept all my dogs in the house, using adequately sized cages for youngsters when necessary, but one cannot really generalise. Different households, different climates, and facilities, and above all what suits the IG and its owner are the criterion. I have seen many homes where the arrangements for the IGs are different to my own, but the dogs have certainly not suffered. I would therefore remind novice readers that the word 'kennel' as used in this context merely means a particular breeder's dogs, not necessarily their living quarters.

COLOUR

When you have decided which breeder or which line you want to purchase from, you may then find that nothing is currently available. Again, I would advise the prospective purchaser to *wait*. I cannot stress sufficiently how foolish it is to rush out and buy the first puppy of the breed that is available, just because it is there. Do not be obsessed by a particular colour. In IGs we have a variety to choose from and we all have our preferences, but remember that when considering a specimen the colour is cosmetic only.

A good judge will always see through colour and markings to the dog itself, and flashy markings can detract as well as improve. One of the ugliest puppies I had was of solid colour and he was a singleton. I thought 'just my luck!' Anyway, he was all there was, so I thought 'I have just got to make the best of it.' He turned out to be Int. & World Dutch & English Ch. Dairylane Moody Blue.

MALE OR FEMALE?

If you are want a puppy to exhibit, I suggest that you consider a male. I know that if a bitch puppy does not come up to expectations you can perhaps improve on her by a litter at a later stage, but believe me, male Italians are lovely to show, and they are nice companions altogether. Bitches sometimes behave rather differently when they are in season and can be independent, whereas most of the males are particularly loving. I know of several exhibitors who share my preference for showing males, if given the choice. There is often more choice available when selecting male puppies because the majority of owners seem to want bitch pups. I know some owners cannot keep males for practical reasons, but I do urge you to think about a male puppy if you are buying your first IG.

If you have decided to purchase a male pup, then you must check to see that the puppy has two testicles. At eight to twelve weeks they will probably not be descended into the scrotum, but they should be visible. At this age they are sometimes very small. Again, if you are a novice you will depend upon the breeder's advice. However, if there is no sign of testicles or only one

The 'ugly duckling': Int. World, Dutch & English Ch. Dairylane Moody Blue at eight weeks.

The 'swan': Int. World, Dutch & English Ch. Dairylane Moody Blue at five months.

appears visible, do not be persuaded to take a chance. Wait until the puppy is a little older or ask the advice of another breeder. A puppy with no testicles or only one testicle will not be a show proposition and should not be used at stud.

BREED POINTS

When the litter is born I am sure you will be desperate to go and see them and hold the precious babies, but most breeders will not welcome you too early. This is because strangers could upset the mother and there is always a risk of infection being brought into the maternity quarters. A good age to see the litter is at eight weeks. At this stage the puppies look like small adults. I always feel that if you like a particular puppy at eight weeks, and you are drawn to it again when it is twelve weeks old, then this is the pup for you.

Watch the puppies running around: even Italian puppies have to stop for breath, and they will pose quite naturally and you will see the length of neck, topline, front and rear end. This will give you a good idea of their 'balance', their general deportment, the carriage of the head and tail, and the general aristocratic stance that is so important to an Italian. When you look at a puppy when it is trotting around, make sure that it can put all four feet to the ground. There must be no sign of any 'skipping' indicating any problems with joints (patella luxation, for instance) on the back legs.

Tail carriage is often high in youngsters, particularly when they are playing, but the tail itself should be nice and long, and reach through the inside of the back legs so as to appear just outside the stifle joint. A shorter tail may often be carried too high when the puppy is at play, but as soon as its demeanour changes to concentrate on more serious pursuits, the tail may fall in the correct way. The IG should eventually carry its tail low, as desired, when in normal adult gait.

Ears are often erratic while teething and at this age I am happy to see 'floppy' ears, i.e. falling over to the front. Ears that are already 'rose-shaped', which is the desired end result, or are flicking up and erect most of the time are cause for concern. There are always exceptions to

Looking at the parents will give a good indication of how a puppy will turn out. Dk. Ch. Il Cagnolino Belizza and her mother Int. Ch. Dk. Ch. Vdh. Ch. Bianca.

Two nice looking Italian Puppies at twelve weeks. Owned by Waltraud Peschges in Germany.

every rule and they *may* finish up OK; but if you are buying in, it is so disappointing if the ears finish up erect, as it spoils the whole appearance and is penalised in the ring. This fault can be bred out in a future generation, but you always have to consider the pedigree carefully if you decide to use a bitch puppy that has this problem. When the time comes to mate her you must be sure to find out as much as possible about the pedigree of the stud dog, to see if you are likely to be doubling up on this fault.

Chunky looking puppies will fine down with age. By this I mean that the rather thick-looking legs will appear finer as the dog grows. A dog's feet are a good guide as to ultimate size; it seems to grow into its feet. Hare feet are the desired type, round cat-like feet are not typical of the breed. The lumpy knee joints are indicative of growth and until these smooth out, growth will continue. Ask the breeder if you can see the dam of the litter, and the sire if he is available, as this will be some guide as to the general ultimate size, although it is not a guarantee. Eyes seem to grow too. The puppy who seems to have small eyes always seems to have bigger eyes as it matures; this is all to do with the overall growth of the head and muzzle.

Blunt-looking muzzles and broad heads usually turn out better than the ones that look like miniature adults, with a small skull and muzzle. The blunt muzzles should mature into long and fine examples, whereas the baby puppy with the adult-looking face and fine bone will in all probability 'finish' much sooner. As a result it will be smaller and finer in all departments than its litter mate, and this often means a smaller head. Fronts will not change, and neither will poor brisket proportions. If you have gone to a responsible and fair breeder they will usually indicate these points to a prospective purchaser; it is of no benefit to the breeder for an owner not to be entirely satisfied with the puppy that is selected.

Ask the breeder to place the puppy on the table for you. Obviously you do not expect it to behave properly, but again some idea of its temperament and general acceptance of handling will be seen, as most sensible breeders start this exercise at three to four weeks of age. I cannot stress enough how important it is to choose a puppy with a happy personality. Of course, you must make allowances for the puppy learning about strange noises, but it should be curious enough to want to come to strangers. All puppies benefit from being used to household noises such as the television and the vacuum cleaner at an early age.

CARING FOR YOUR PUPPY

Hopefully, one of the things that will have attracted you to a particular litter or line will be the coats and skins of the parents, which is a very important factor in the breed. Initially this is bred for, but then it is up to you, the new owner, to maintain the coat in top-class condition, and this applies equally to all aspects of the dog's health and well-being. I have found that providing soft bedding for the dog to lie on, plus another soft blanket for the dog to cover itself with, helps the Italian's coat to be clean at all times and is much more successful than constant bathing. It is not necessary to use oils and sprays or other artificial aids, unless a dog has lost its jacket during the winter months or through illness or old age.

Good food is essential. You only get out of an Italian what goes in. Check on the diet given by the breeder and then if you feel that you can improve on it, do so. Basically, you should be feeding good meat – either fresh or canned – and biscuit, plus cereal and milk substitute in the early stages, and whatever additives you have been advised by the breeder or your vet. Remember that too many additives are as bad as too few. Try to keep the pup well covered, almost fat; a puppy burns up so much energy that it runs off the fat. If, for some reason, you decide on a different diet for the puppy, do not introduce the change immediately. Give the little one a few days of eating the food it is used to while it settles into its new home.

I often feel that when puppies change homes, no matter how happy they are, they do have a slight set-back in their growth. They seem big and plump when they first arrive, and they seem to stop growing or slow up during this changeover period. This is only a personal opinion, but I have seen it happen so many times that I am quite sure it occurs. It is essential for puppies to have rest periods, especially after meals. Puppies are like children and they will keep on and on playing and running about until they are exhausted. Sleep is just as essential a part of the puppy's day as play.

When you leave the breeder and take responsibility for your precious puppy, this is when you start on its preparation if you hope to be successful in the show ring. The good breeding should be there, but you must supply the good feeding, fresh air, exercise, warm bed, clean blankets, plus lots and lots of love and attention. All the additives in the world will not make up for these last ingredients. Purchase your puppy, love your puppy – above all, respect your puppy.

If you are a working owner, try to arrange a vacation so that you do not have to leave the puppy on its own immediately. Older dogs will accept this situation, but a new puppy will feel totally abandoned. The accessories required for the Italian should already have been purchased before the little one arrives, i.e. collar, lead, blankets, and bed. A crate is also of value, not only in the home but also for travelling and at shows. If the puppy gets used to it for short periods it will quickly accept it as its own mobile home. Lastly, if you have purchased your Italian Greyhound hoping to exhibit it, remember that you are in the show ring for about five minutes, but you live with your Italian, and your conscience, for the rest of the time.

BREEDING CONTRACTS

All breeders should provide registration papers and a pedigree. Most will sell a youngster without any contracts involved; but if you have made some agreement such as a breeding contract, then do make sure you understand all that it implies. You do not want to feel you *must* breed from a bitch, for instance, before you are sure she is mature enough, nor do you want to rear a litter at a time when it is inconvenient to you, the owner. You will be responsible for finding suitable homes for all the puppies, and this could be a problem if you have a lot of male puppies. Can you have a puppy back, or an adult, if it should fall on unfortunate times? All responsible breeders must make this provision, and so breeding a litter is a very longterm responsibility. Beautiful friendships have been broken because of breeding contracts, as well as made, so do consider all angles.

Chapter Four

PREPARING FOR THE RING

When the litter is about three to four weeks of age it is a good idea to handle the puppies a little bit more. Obviously the breeder will have been touching the pups with warm clean hands in the normal course of events prior to this, i.e. changing bedding, early weaning, etc. It is not wise to intrude too much on the mother's domain and bother her. However, at this later age one can certainly hold the puppy up on a table, just for a few minutes, talking gently to it. This early association with being handled on higher level than is normal certainly pays off.

As the puppy starts to stand more firmly on its four legs it should be handled in this way two or three times a day, and the 'table training' of its show career commenced. It is always useful to offer some small morsel of food as a reward; something that will not upset the small insides of the young one. Much praise is always necessary at all times during the training sessions. I cannot stress sufficiently that a puppy should never be left on the table if some interruption should occur. Always put the puppy back safely in its pen or back on to the floor. In fact, it is often wise to use a table or surface that is not in the immediate vicinity of the puppy's usual living quarters in case it tries to have a go on its own.

When you are holding the puppy in place on the table, you can gently push your finger around the mouth area to get the little one used to the fact that a stranger will be doing this at a later stage to look at its teeth. However, do be careful during the teething time as the gums will be very tender. Enrol members of the family or visitors to 'go over' a puppy from time to time so that it gets used to being handled by strangers.

A word of advice here: when your puppy is ready for its first vaccination and you take the puppy to the vet, do avoid, if at all possible, placing the pup on the vet's table for examination. Most vets are very reasonable if this request is put to them politely. The problem is that any unpleasant experience, such as an injection or similar, can remain in the mind of a puppy for quite a while, and this could instil a fear of being placed on the table, which would be disastrous for a show prospect. The majority of vets will be quite happy for you to hold the youngster in your arms.

As the puppy gets a little bigger, run your hand over its back and down its tail and hocks. Never get cross with the trainee, even if you feel like it, as IGs can be very stubborn. Many pups behave perfectly well for a week or two, and then they adopt a new attitude and move every foot, four times a second! If you have a youngster with a tendency to lean away from you, I suggest you go around the other side of the puppy and stand it from that side. If you try to steady the puppy all the time you will never cure this annoying habit.

Equally, if a puppy will not stand upright, the best solution is to stand in front of the pup at the head-end and place its front feet with a little to spare at the edge of the table. Obviously the IG will not want to fall off, and if you are safely in front of it, then it cannot, but it will realise that it has to stand still to be sure of its ground. Never train on the table for too long; little and often should be the motto. On days when nothing is going right, forget it. Never finish on a bad note; it is important that both you and the puppy enjoy these sessions.

LEASH TRAINING

Personally I do not make too much of a thing about leash training. I find on the occasions when I have tried the puppy on the lead in the garden it usually is a bit of a battle. I might play at it for a day or two, just so that the puppy knows what the lead feels like. Some breeders feel that a light cat-collar or similar is beneficial to wear for short periods. Generally, I find that if you wait until your puppy is fully inoculated against the infectious diseases it will happily accept the idea of a lead when it is out on the street or somewhere else.

It is always more interesting for the puppy to be going somewhere interesting rather than just walking backwards and forwards in the garden, and it will forget about the lead because it is so curious about its surroundings. I find that if lead training is started in this way, both dog and owner will enjoy the outings. I have found that it often helps if you can take another older dog with you, as this can be a great morale booster for the little IG making its first foray into the outside world.

When you are walking your puppy anywhere outside the confines of the garden you must ensure that it is wearing a collar and lead of the correct style with a name disc attached; an ordinary show or slip lead is not sufficient. Most exhibitors prefer a nylon slip lead or a very fine check chain in the show ring, but apart from the safety aspect, it is better for the IG to know the difference between the 'going out' collar and lead and the 'show lead'. There is certain behaviour that is tolerated when a dog is out for a walk, which would be unacceptable in the show ring. Therefore the sooner the dog makes the distinction, the better – and it is surprising how quickly they learn that when the show lead goes on they are in 'showing mode'!

SHOW TRAINING CLASSES

When the puppy is four to five months old you can get a little more organised in a show training routine. Find out if there are any local show training (ringcraft) classes in the neighbourhood. There will be a mixture of breeds, and you must make sure that your IG does not feel threatened or overpowered by the environment. However, you should find that there is plenty of sensible advice and encouragement available for novice owners.

A word of warning, however, do make sure the people responsible for organising the training are used to smaller dogs, as it is possible to do more harm than good. Judges, trainers, and anyone else, no matter how well intentioned, can be far too heavy-handed if they are not used to IGs, and thus your future show dog can be ruined by unfortunate mishandling. Puppies have long memories, and an unpleasant experience at this stage can be very difficult to erase.

Remember to give lots of praise all the way along. Never make the training sessions, even at the proper classes, continue for too long. If you feel your puppy is beginning to get bored, then excuse yourself from the proceedings. A young Italian who finds the training boring will not learn anything. Each dog is an individual and has to be treated as such. Some methods used on one will not work on another. Experienced owners often find they can do the basics at home and the progressive stages seem to come naturally.

However, it should always be remembered that while a good handler can enhance the appearance of a not so good puppy, a poor handler can spoil the chances of a good puppy, just by the fact that it is difficult to assess. With the ever-rising cost of entering dog shows, it makes sense to present a dog as well as possible. All good judges make allowances for the misbehaviour of puppies – nobody wants to see a row of stuffed dummies at such a tender age – but if a dog absolutely refuses to stand on the table, or walk in a semblance of a straight line, how can the person adjudicating the class be expected to assess its worth?

ROAD WALKING
Any faults in the construction of a dog cannot, of course, be altered, and these will inevitably govern the dog's stance and movement. However, if the dog appears to turn back legs in or out, or to be untidy in some other aspect of movement, I believe that this can certainly be helped considerably by road walking. Youngsters obviously need to have plenty of free running exercise to develop muscles etc., but controlled walking on a lead can do wonders.

I also believe that more than one dog walked together in this way on a regular basis is not a good idea. The dogs tend to jostle each other, and the one on the outside tends to turn slightly inwards, and the inside dog turns outwards. If there are several dogs on leads, this situation is multiplied. In my opinion, it is best to walk a show dog on its own at a good, even gait on a very regular basis, and over the months you will be able to see considerable improvement. No puppy should be allowed to over-exercise; all growing youngsters should be encouraged to have rest periods, but the length of time that they can be walked should be increased as time goes by.

MOVING YOUR IG
In the ring, the judge will usually ask exhibitors to move their dogs in a 'triangle' or sometimes in a 'T' and to move up and down. The dog will also be examined on the table. Always listen to the instructions given by the judge, and move as indicated. Remember to keep a keen eye on the judge, as well as keeping your attention on your dog, as it is essential to keep the dog between yourself and the judge at all times. Practise to make sure that you do not end up by getting tangled up with the lead – it is the dog the judge wishes to see moving, not your legs!

Practise either stacking your dog or free standing it at home or at show training classes. When you lift your exhibit from the table after the judge has examined it, take your time to get the lead and collar where you want it, and often your IG will shake itself too. Get your IG's attention by whatever means you have practised at home, and do not be in such a hurry that you waste the time available by rushing off with the dog shaking and the lead all over the place.

Adjust your speed to suit your dog – this is something that you should have practised at home. A mirror can be a very useful aid, as then the owner can see things from the judge's perspective and amend handling procedures accordingly. During the 'moving' exercise the show lead should either be allowed to hang loosely at the side of the dog's neck, or held upwards. When the lead is held up, the collar should just tighten at the end of the jawbone; it should not be over the adam's apple, and the dog must not look as if it is about to choke. Nobody wishes to see the dog's front feet lifted off the ground or see it being dragged along. However, this method, if executed correctly, gives the dog a cleaner outline. If the lead is hanging loosely it will touch the dog's shoulder from time to time, and this may affect its movement.

The final choice is yours, and it depends upon the personality of your dog. The owner's hand should be held away from the body to give the dog its own space to present itself. Do not pull the dog closely alongside you, as would be required in an Obedience competition. Remember you are there to show off your dog, so always feel proud of what you have at the end of the lead – do not appear to be apologising for being there! You may find, particularly with a youngster, that you will need to change your tactics depending upon the mood of the dog and the weather, if it is an outdoor show. Sometimes if you bend or kneel to stack the dog it will seem to fold up, whereas if you remain standing and have sufficient rapport with your dog, it will stand much better, in a more relaxed way and will look the nicer for it.

Those in other breeds always assume that the Italian must be a very easy dog to show. Those of us that have done it know better – an IG can be very stubborn! If an Italian is not in the mood, nobody is going to get it to show off its undoubted charms, and I have seen many an experienced handler setting and resetting their dear little IG who has decided "not today, thank you!"

BAITING

If you decide to 'bait' your dog, i.e. using a tasty titbit to make your dog look alert at a particular point in the proceedings, such as when you have finished your triangle and are standing in front of the judge, with the dog posed naturally, this is in order, provided it is unobtrusive. Never let the titbit intrude into your performance; the few minutes you are allowed to actually 'present' your Italian seem to go by in a flash. There is nothing worse than seeing pieces of meat thrust at a dog at all stages, which happens with some breeds. Not only does this look awful, but it results in other exhibits sniffing and pulling to get to the food.

In fact, the art of baiting is not necessarily to *give* your exhibit the food, but to let it *think* you are going to! In other words, if the judge is *not* looking at your dog, you could allow it to have a tasty morsel from your pocket. Then, when the judge *is* looking at your dog, just move your hand to the pocket where the food is contained, or move your hand within your pocket, and this will have the desired effect of attracting your dog's attention, without causing annoyance or making your dog too fidgety; it will have its eyes fixed on you, in the hope of what it may get. The trick is to form a relationship with your dog so that it is so intent on watching you to see what is required, it will totally disregard anything else going on either inside or outside the show ring.

THE FINAL ASSESSMENT

After the judge has examined your dog and seen it move, return to your place. You should allow the IG to relax for a few minutes with lots of praise and fuss, and perhaps one of those little titbits. Keep your eye on the proceedings, however, and as the final dog is moving, begin to position your dog.

The exhibits will be lined up after the judge has assessed them all individually, and then placements will be made. Again, make use of the space available, do not get too close to the other exhibitors and make sure your dog's attention if focused on you. Always take winning and losing in good spirit, and remember to congratulate the winners if you are not so fortunate; it is always a nice feeling to be on the receiving end of this behaviour. Unfortunately there are occasionally those exhibitors who are less than gracious in defeat, but this does them no credit, and is less than a credit to the breed.

THE HANDLER'S PRESENTATION

It does help if you consider the clothes you are going to wear when you exhibit your dog. A neatly turned out combination of dog and handler is pleasant to see, whether the handler is a man or a woman. Women obviously have more choice of attire, and this can lead to problems. Long skirts must not impede or flap in the front of the dog when it is moving, and lower heels are more sensible than high heels so that you can move smoothly alongside the dog, without distracting it. High heels clacking on an inside floor are a real annoyance for a dog, and I have seen them look quite apprehensive, as well they may, for the danger of being stepped on is not to be under-estimated.

The colour of clothing can complement your dog, but it can also mar the dog's appearance. A woman wearing a gaudy floral dress standing beside a white trimmed dog can spoil the outline; equally 'matching' the colour of your clothes to the dog will make it blend in with you, rather than stand out in the ring. The fawn-coloured dogs often look well against black, and blue dogs look good against red; it is worth thinking about this aspect. It does not always seem apparent to you close up in the ring, but from the ringside or when the judge is watching you move it can make a difference. If you are using titbits it is useful to have a pocket for this, and other essential things. Some breeders, particularly in the United States, employ a professional handler to present their dog, and obviously they will not have to worry about this aspect as the professionals are already highly skilled in the art of presentation.

THE IG'S PRESENTATION

Your Italian Greyhound should be taken into the ring in its usual immaculate jacket, with nails trimmed. Teeth should have been cleaned as part of its normal routine. A clean show lead is a must. Your ring card showing your exhibit number should be attached to your person with clip or band, as preferred. Some owners like to trim the whiskers on their Italian to give a neat appearance, and some say it enhances the muzzle. Others feel it is not natural to cut off these sensory powers; you must decide for yourself. When I am judging, it does not influence me one way or the other. You can always compromise by cutting off the long eyebrows and the whiskers on the moles on the cheeks and underneath the jaw, and leave the rest as they are.

If you decide to trim, be very careful and hold the IG steadily and firmly, or get someone else to hold the dog while you cut. You may well find that you think you have made a very neat job of trimming the whiskers, and as soon as the IG is released you will see that they look awful. An IG seems to be able to lay these whiskers back flat against the muzzle, and nothing looks worse than black stubble! The tail can also be enhanced by trimming if it is very hairy underneath. Trim the surfeit of hair, using the scissors with the blades used flat, underneath the tail and along the side, to give a neat and rat-like appearance. Give your dog a quick polish with a piece of silk or velvet, and you are ready for the ring.

These preparations of trimming should be done at home in the quiet of your own surroundings. IGs that have a lot of white on them will have to be bathed or the white parts, at least, will need to be washed. You can only discover by trial and error to see how a bath affects the coat, and whether it needs to be done a few days before the show to allow the natural oils to do their work. A light dusting of scurf can sometimes result immediately after bathing, which is obviously undesirable. Novice exhibitors should always take the time to study the Kennel Club rules governing the Exhibition of Dogs. Time spent before you commence can avoid many embarrassing situations later. Experienced exhibitors and the Secretaries of the Breed Clubs should always be willing to help; if you don't know something, never be afraid to ask. It is also a good idea to visit several shows before you actually begin to exhibit your first Italian.

Before you enter the ring, give your Italian a chance to stretch its legs. A few minutes making sure the IG is comfortable, giving it the opportunity to relieve itself, and a quick reminder of the moving on the lead procedure will be time well spent. One of the essential items in your pocket is a 'wipe'. Male IGs have an awful habit of managing to urinate all over their stomachs, legs and feet, just before entering the ring. Bright yellow stain is not nice to look at, and even less attractive when you have to pick up your exhibit. These disposable wipes are very handy for last-minute cleaning up. Chalk and talcum powder are also useful cleaning agents and there are many other proprietary items on the market at the shows. However, there is a general tightening up on the use of grooming aids by the governing bodies, and you should always make sure that nothing remains on the dog's coat other than its own natural sheen.

Make sure you avoid rushing into the ring at the last minute; if you do, your Italian will probably have its tail up in the air, and will be in too frisky a mood to co-operate. Always use the same words of command in the ring that you have used in practice, whatever formula works between you two. Even the most seasoned exhibitor gets a little dry in the mouth and excited just before entering the ring, and if this enthusiasm wanes I think you should retire from exhibiting dogs. However, it is vital to remember that the dog you take into the ring is the same one you bring out, whether it achieves a placing or not. You and your little IG are a team, and to you, it is always a winner!

32

Chapter Five

THE BREED STANDARD

The Breed Standard is the template that breeders and judges aim to comply with in order to produce and assess typical specimens of the breed in question. As a breeder I know that "The best laid schemes o' mice an' men gang aft a-gley" (Robert Burns), and sometimes the current puppy 'waiting in the wings' is not really quite as I had hoped for. If your previous exhibit has proved highly successful in the show ring, it is always difficult to follow on with a new dog without being aware of the comparison with the former. Sometimes there may be a particular point that could be better, but if the overall picture is good and the dog and handler are working in harmony this may still prove a winning combination. The same situation arises when judging dogs. The judge may not be entirely happy about all aspects of the exhibit that is awarded first prize, but there is no such thing as a perfect specimen, and both judge and breeder must learn to assess the animal as a whole.

In l900 The Italian Greyhound Club in the UK first devised a system of points for judging the breed based on an original scale drawn up in l859/60. Very little has ever been done to change the basic requirements, apart from the 'size' and 'colour' stipulations. The 1900 Standard stipulated: "Two classes; one of seven pounds and under and one over seven pounds and not exceeding eleven." The weight clause was amended to eight pounds instead of seven a little later. The words "high stepping and free" were also included and special trophies were awarded for the dog with the best 'action' at several shows. The colour section originally read: "Preferably self-coloured. The colour most prized is golden fawn, but all shades of fawn, red, mouse, blue, cream and white, are recognised, and blacks, brindle, and pied are considered less desirable." In l909 the system of points was dropped. The section referring to colour was also amended to allow less emphasis on the whole-coloured dog with the addition: "Faults – Black or Blue with Tan markings."

In 1949 after consultation with all the various Breed Clubs that had by now evolved, the Kennel Club in the UK decided to publish the Standards for all the breeds. The next alteration to the Breed Standard for the Italian Greyhound came in 1962 when the Breed Club decided to add the word 'brindle' under the list of 'Faults'. This was to ensure absolutely pure breeding in Italian Greyhounds as there were a few still experimenting with cross-breeding. The Whippet was very popular and some tried to alter sizes by mixing the two, i.e. attempting to make the IG bigger and the Whippet smaller, and vice versa. Even today IG owners still occasionally suffer from the onlooker who confuses their prized Italian with a Whippet. However, to the knowledgeable, the differences between a Greyhound, an Italian Greyhound and a Whippet are only too apparent.

The strict adherence to the colour faults meant that any intrusion of these faulty colours would automatically preclude these dogs from serious breeders' pedigrees, as the faulty colouring intimated the cross-breeding with terriers, particularly Black and Tans, and Manchesters. This was such a waste, in my opinion, when some of the pedigrees were so old and valuable. To suggest that this did not matter is foolish, as even in the last few years I have personally known of Italian Greyhounds being born with faulty colouring. Edward C. Ash, writing in l938, stated: "It is not wise to dogmatize on how little influence previous ancestry exerts. I remember the birth in my herd of cattle, of a dun calf. I suppose the last dun ancestor lived eighty to a hundred years ago....."

In the UK the Standard was to remain the same until l986 when the Kennel Club decided that the various Breed Standards should have some uniformity and urged Breed Clubs to use the same headings and to describe in more detail, yet concisely, the points required. The following is the current Breed Standard as used nowadays. It was never the intention of the breeders involved in revamping the Standard to change it, or the breed, in any way.

THE BRITISH BREED STANDARD

GENERAL APPEARANCE A greyhound in miniature, more slender in all proportions.

CHARACTERISTICS Elegant, graceful and quick moving.

TEMPERAMENT Intelligent, affectionate and vivacious, may appear aloof.

HEAD & SKULL Skull long, flat and narrow, slight stop. Muzzle fine and long. Nose dark in colour.

EYES Rather large, bright; full of expression.

EARS Rose-shaped, placed well back, soft and fine, not pricked.

MOUTH Jaws strong, with a perfect, regular and complete scissor bite, i.e. the upper teeth closely overlapping the lower teeth and set square to the jaws. Teeth even.

NECK Long, gracefully arched.

FOREQUARTERS Shoulders long and sloping. Legs straight; well set under shoulders; fine, strong bone and pasterns.

BODY Chest deep and narrow. Good length of rib and brisket. Back slightly arched over loin.

HINDQUARTERS Long, well muscled thigh: hind legs parallel when viewed from behind; well bent stifle, hocks well let down.

FEET Hare feet.

TAIL Low set, long, fine, carried low.

GAIT/MOVEMENT High stepping and free action. Front and hind legs to move forward as in a straight line with propulsion from behind.

COAT Skin fine and supple. Hair, short, fine and glossy.

COLOUR Black, blue, cream, fawn, red, white, or any of these colours broken with white. White dogs may be broken with one of these colours. Black or blue with tan markings, or brindle not acceptable.

SIZE Ideal height 32-38 cms ($12^{1}/_{2}$-15 ins) at withers. Ideal weight 3.6-4.5 kgs (8-10 lbs). Overall type and elegance essential.

FAULTS Any departure from the foregoing points should be considered a fault and the seriousness with which the fault should be regarded should be in exact proportion to its degree.

NOTE Male animals should have two apparently normal testicles fully descended into the scrotum.
Reproduced by kind permission of the English Kennel Club (revised November 1998).

Italian Greyhounds were first registered with the American Kennel Club in 1886 and their current Breed Standard is as follows:

THE AMERICAN BREED STANDARD

DESCRIPTION The Italian Greyhound is very similar to the Greyhound, but much smaller and more slender in all proportions and of ideal elegance and grace.

HEAD Narrow and long, tapering to nose, with a slight suggestion of stop.

SKULL Rather long, almost flat.

MUZZLE Long and fine.

NOSE Dark. It may be black or brown or in keeping with the colour of the dog. A light or partly pigmented nose is a fault.

TEETH Scissors bite. A badly undershot or overshot mouth is a fault.

EYES Dark, bright, intelligent, medium in size. Very light eyes are a fault.

EARS Small, fine in texture; thrown back and folded except when alerted, then carried folded at right angles to the head. Erect or button ears severely penalized.

NECK Long, slender and gracefully arched.

BODY Of medium length, short coupled; high at withers, back curved and drooping at hindquarters, the highest point of curve at start of loin, creating a definite tuck up at flanks.

SHOULDERS Long and sloping.

CHEST Deep and narrow.

FORELEGS Long, straight, set well under shoulder; strong pasterns, fine bone.

HINDQUARTERS Long, well muscled thigh; hind legs parallel when viewed from behind, hocks well let down, well bent stifle.

FEET Hare foot with well arched toes. Removal of dew claws optional.

TAIL Slender and tapering to a curve end, long enough to reach the hock; set low, carried low. Ring tail a serious fault, gay tail a fault.

COAT Skin, fine and supple, hair short, glossy like satin and soft to the touch.

COLOR Any color and markings are acceptable except that a dog with brindle markings and a dog with the tan markings normally found on black and tan dogs of other breeds must be disqualified.

ACTION High stepping and free, front and hind legs to move forward in a straight line.

SIZE Height at withers, ideally 13 to 15 inches.

DISQUALIFICATION A dog with brindle markings or a dog with the tan markings normally found on black and tan dogs of other breeds.

Reproduced by kind permission of the American Kennel Club (1993).

Europe, Argentina, Mexico, Peru, Japan, Venezuela, San Marino Republique, Gibraltar, San Salvador and Panama all currently hold dog shows under the jurisdiction of the Federation Cynologique Internationale (FCI) governing body, whose headquarters are in Belgium. In the UK, USA and Australia we refer to Challenge Certificates (CCs); in the FCI countries winning dogs are awarded Certificat d'Aptitude au Championat (CAC) to attain their Championship titles and Certificat d'Aptitude au Championat International de Beaute (CACIB) to attain International Championships. Australia has recently become affiliated to the FCI; however, it is not yet clear what changes to the Breed Standard and to the show award system might be introduced in order to conform to the FCI. The FCI Breed Standard has important differences from the UK and American Breed Standards, particularly in relation to colour. There has been concern shown by some Continental judges with regard to the differences between the FCI Standard and the British and American Standards. The sighthound judge Piero Renai della Rena wrote the following in the dog press: "A breed that in its country of origin is officially placed among the sighthounds MUST necessarily have all the characteristics common to the members of this group: conformation, elegance, strength, and an elastic, untiring movement. Refined and graceful of course – but without weakness and free from faults that would reduce its efficiency. No sighthound could be different and still be called a sighthound. Its height, maximum 15 inches and minimum 13 inches: its colour, solid (grey, blue, black or fawn) – rose ears – a straight topline with arched loins, and consequently an inclined croup and low set tail – scapula/humerus angle rather open. All these points are of fundamental importance because with the crested neck they determine the characteristic movement."

In my opinion, this is exactly what *all* IG enthusiasts are aiming for, but perhaps it is in the translation of one language to another that problems arise. For instance the words 'straight topline' in the UK tends to be interpreted as meaning 'level' topline, like that of a Chihuahua, perhaps. However, the picture used to illustrate these words had the 'normal' topline, with a rise over the loin, which is what judges in the UK and elsewhere also hope to find.

FCI BREED STANDARD

BRIEF HISTORICAL SUMMARY The small Italian Greyhound is descended from the short Greyhound or small (waisted) Greyhound which was already in existence in ancient Egypt in the court of the Pharoahs. In by-passing the Greek Laconites, where a number of visual representations were made on vases and tombs, the breed first appeared in Italy during the 5th century. The breed's development took place during the Renaissance period in the households of the nobility. It is not uncommon to find the Italian Greyhound depicted on the pictures of the greatest Italian masters and other artists.

GENERAL APPEARANCE Rangy appearance. The trunk is joined in the square and its shape in miniature is reminiscent of those of Greyhounds and of the Sloughi. It is a model of grace and distinction.

IMPORTANT PROPORTIONS The length is equal to or at least less than the height of the withers. The length of the skull is equal to half the length of the head. The length of the head could be up to 40 per cent of the height of the withers.

BEHAVIOUR AND CHARACTER Reserved, affectionate and docile.

HEAD Shape elongated and thin. The length could extend to 40 per cent of the withers.

THE SKULL Skull flat, tapering along its length. The length of the skull is equal to half

the length of the head. Region under the orbit well defined.

STOP Frontal depression not very noticeable.

NOSE Of a dark colour, preferably black with well opened nostrils.

MUZZLE The tip, and the edges of the lips to have well darkened pigmentation, fine lips set firmly on the jaw.

JAW Elongated, with the incisors well aligned when running, robust in relation to the size of the dog.

CHEEKS Lean.

TEETH Complete, and healthy dentition. Teeth should be firmly in place, at right angles to the jaw; scissor bite.

EYES Big and expressive, with eyeballs neither deep-set nor bulging out. Iris of a dark colour. Rim of the pupils pigmented.

EARS Attached quite high, small with thin cartilage. The ears fold back on themselves and lean back on the nape of the neck and on the highest point of the neck. When the dog is on the alert, the base of the ear stands up and the distal part tightens both laterally and horizontally – position commonly known as "en auvent" (or roofed).

NECK
Profile: Slightly arched and joined at the base near the withers.
Length of neck: Equal to that of the head.
Form: Truncated cone shape, well muscled.

SKIN Fits closely over frame without tautness.

BODY The length is equal or slightly less than the height of the withers.
Topline: Straight profile with an arched back lumbar region. The lumbar curvature runs harmoniously in line with the croup.

WITHERS: Quite pronounced.

BACK Straight, well muscled with a deep chest, descending to the elbows.

HINDQUARTERS/CROUP Very strong, wide and well muscled.

CHEST Narrow.

TAIL Attached low down, fine even at the root, it becomes progressively finer until the tip.

It is carried low and straight for the first half of its length and then curves up. It must be long enough to allow it, when passed between the lower limbs and pulled up high, to jut out a little from the haunch. The hair is short.

FOREQUARTERS Altogether good structure, with sound muscles.

SHOULDERS Slightly oblique with a well developed set of muscles, distinct and prominent.

FRONT LEGS With a very open joint between the shoulder blades and the humerus: in a parallel direction in the middle of the body.

ELBOWS Neither sticking out not pointing inwards.

FOREARM The length of the measured limb from the ground to the elbow is barely that of the elbow to the withers; very light frame; forearm in perfect vertical position looking as good from the front as from the profile.

PASTERNS In the continuation of the vertical line from the forearm, from the profile view, it is slightly oblique (diagonal).

FEET Almost oval in shape, small with arched toes and good joints. Small pigmented plantar pads. Nails black or darkened in accordance with the colour of the coat at the feet where white would be tolerated.

HINDQUARTERS Altogether and rear view, perfectly balanced, perfect composure.

THIGHS Wide, solid, not voluminous, with well defined muscles.

HINDLEGS Very oblique with a fine bone apparent and a good legging groove. Good angulation. (The skin is almost transparent in the lower part of the legs and the tendons are clearly visible.)

STIFLE AND HOCK These are located along an imaginary vertical line continued from the point of the buttocks.

FEET Less oval than the front feet, with arched toes and good joints; small plantar pads and nails well pigmented as at the front.

GAIT Springy, harmonious, without being raised. Quick free canter with a spring or thrust in the step.

SKIN Thin and well applied (close fitting) on all regions of the body with the exception of the elbows where it is more tightly drawn.

COAT The hair is short and fine on all the body without any trace of fringes.

COLOUR Uniform colour of black, grey, slate grey, slate and fawn (Isabella in Italian) in all possible shades and nuances. White is only tolerated on the chest and feet.

SIZE AND WEIGHT
Height at withers: Male and female from 32cms to 38 cms.

Weight: Male and female 5 kg maximum.

FAULTS All deviations from the descriptions which precede constitute a fault, which in judging will be penalised in accordance with the gravity and the extent. These descriptions apply equally to dogs which always amble and those which have raised gaits (harpee, trussed, raised steps). (Amble – similar to pacing; harpee – as playing a harp; egg beating – legs lift and pasterns flick inwards.)

FAULTS TO BE PENALISED Accentuated convergence or divergence of the axis of the facial cranium. Nose totally or half-discoloured (not pigmented). Concave or convex bevelling of the nose, dewclaw, raised bottom on the back, coat of more than one colour, white skin outside the indicated sections (breast and feet) for the acceptable Standard. Smaller size than 32 cms or larger than 38 cms for males or females.

FAULTS WHICH DISQUALIFY Under or overshot jaws, different coloured eyes, total lack of pigmentation around the edges of the pupils, tail-less or docked, if they are congenital abnormalities.

NB Males must have two testicles completely descended in the scrotum and of normal appearance.

The FCI Breed Standard is reproduced with the permission of the Secretariat General in Belgium.

Standard No. 200. Issued 30th March 1992.
Translation from Italian to French by Dr J. M. Paschoud in collaboration with Dr A. Roncarati.
Origin: Italy.
Classification: Group 10, sect. 3. Short-haired sighthounds.
Date of Publication 27th November 1989.
Translated from French to English by Judith Barton, June 1992.(Amendments to include canine terminology are the sole responsibility of the author.)

INTERPRETING THE REQUIREMENTS OF THE BREED STANDARDS
It would be nice to think that all breeds of dog looked the same all over the world but, sad to say, this is not the case in many breeds. This is only too apparent when photographs are compared. However, I think that generally there is a fair comparison in Italian Greyhounds. At different shows, on different days, in any country, you can get the impression the breed has 'improved' or

has 'taken a turn for the worse', but in the main the IG is the same everywhere. Colour, size and movement are probably the main cause of disagreement arising from the different requirements in the Breed Standards, i.e. USA/UK and the FCI. Let us take the points one by one and I will do my best to give my own impression of their meaning.

GENERAL APPEARANCE

This is universal. An Italian Greyhound must look *elegant* before all else. The description – greyhound in miniature is quite apt, and the graceful yet quick movement is typical of all countries.

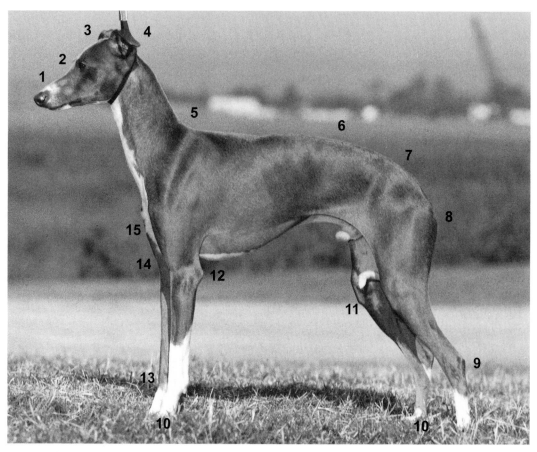

Points of anatomy. Ch. Littleleluv's Sherlock Holmes. Owned by K. Holmes.

KEY

1. Muzzle	6. Topline	11. Stifle
2. Stop	7. Hindquarters	12. Elbow
3. Skull	8. Low tail carriage	13. Pasterns
4. Rose ears	9. Hock	14. Brisket
5. Shoulders	10. Long hare feet	15. Deep, narrow chest

TEMPERAMENT

You need to know the breed in order to appreciate the temperament. Nervousness, which I interpret as a total refusal to be handled, attempting to bite, etc. is not to be tolerated – neither in the ring nor as a future parent. However the aloof nature of an IG is an entirely different manner. An IG will often duck out of the way if a stranger reaches out to touch it when out in the street, and until a dog becomes experienced this can happen in the show ring. The intelligent little face will sometimes put on an air of absolute disdain, as if to indicate it is far too important to speak to a stranger. Others are very forward and outgoing and love everybody at home, but it is a different matter when they are in a strange environment.

Experienced breed judges appreciate this and allow time for the IG to settle and 'get their bearings'. It is important to remember that an Italian Greyhound has exceptionally fine skin, and the sudden laying on of hands (particularly if they are cold ones) by some judges, perhaps used to more robust breeds, must feel very uncomfortable. By their very inborn nature, IGs are happy and loving companions, but this aloof manner – quite distinct from aggression or bad temperament – is a natural reaction and typical of many hounds. Puppies that are destined for the show ring are expected to get over any nerves as soon as possible in order show off their qualities.

LEFT: Three Italians showing correct heads, correct eyes and correct ears.

Neal.

BELOW: Incorrect: apple head and bulbous eyes, particularly the dog pictured right.

HEAD AND SKULL

The head must not be as broad between the ears as that of a Whippet. A moderately long and narrow foreface is desired, but this must include a slight rise from the centre point just below the eye line to the occiput, without making the dog 'apple headed'. It is nice to see overall a 'feminine' or 'masculine' face, and the more contrast that is apparent between the sexes, the more attractive the Italian Greyhound will be.

EYES

I believe that the eyes on all dogs make or break their whole facial appearance. An Italian with nice bright eyes, fairly large – but not bulbous or prominent – can almost 'smile' with its eyes. The whole face and expression is really governed by this feature. The pigment on the eye rims should emphasise their colour, and some appear to have eye-liner worn 'Cleopatra' style. In some pale fawn dogs the pigment is rather lacking and the eye rims tend to be paler.

NOSE

The only mention of pigment in the Breed Standards refers to the nose, but generally the colour of the dog rules the pigment. Black or brown in keeping with the colour of the dog is acceptable, but a very light pink nose or one that is partly pink in colour is not so agreeable and should be penalised by judges. The genetics that govern the colour of the dog obviously affect pigmentation, and this also applies to the colour of the dog's nails and pads.

Two Italians showing correct ear carriage: left 'laid back', right 'alert' ('en auvent'; 'a tetto').

Bjorch.

EARS

These should be carried in a rose-shaped position, which means they are folded halfway along, and this folds on to itself. The ears should be small and feel thin to the touch; the skin should not feel thick or leathery. When a dog is standing in repose the ears will fold back along the side of the head. If a dog is really startled it may put its ears up in an erect position momentarily, until they fall back to their normal carriage.

When a dog arises from sleep its ears are often warm and floppy, but regularly erratic ear carriage or permanently floppy 'button' ear carriage is an extremely unattractive fault and will be penalised heavily in the ring. An owner is unwise to ignore this detail in any young prospect for the show ring. However, 'teething allowances' are made for problems in this department. By

Incorrect:
'button'
ears.

Puppies will often
have erratic ear
carriage,
particularly when
teething.

this I mean that while the IG is cutting new teeth, ear carriage can be affected, but as the exhibit gets older this fault is less likely to be overlooked. Many judges rattle something or click their tongue to get the dog's attention while it is standing in the ring, and if the exhibit has irregular, pricked ear carriage it will soon be apparent.

MOUTH
The explanation in the Breed Standard concerning the mouth of an Italian Greyhound is self-explanatory. A correctly shaped mouth and jaw line will have a correct muzzle shape. Those that are slightly overshot, a fault often seen in hound-type breeds, tend to have insufficient underjaw. This is not attractive and makes the muzzle appear snipey. I think it fair to say that those judges and exhibitors governed by the FCI Breed Standard probably pay far more attention to the dentition than is considered necessary by others.

In smaller examples of the breed it is not uncommon to find that one or two premolars are missing, yet the rest of the teeth are set correctly and the bite is as it should be. A judge that is not guided by the FCI Standard may be aware of this slight deficiency, but may consider the overall quality of the dog far outweighs this point and award a prize accordingly. However, a judge who complies with the FCI Standard is less likely to ignore this 'fault'. Personal views

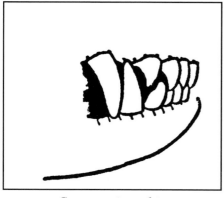

Correct scissor bite

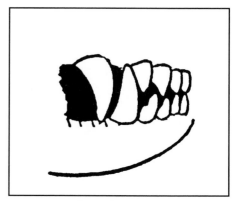

Imperfect edge-to-edge bite

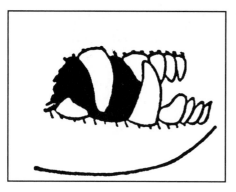

Faulty undershot jaw
(Top teeth inside bottom teeth)

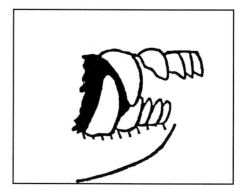

Faulty overshot jaw
(Top teeth well over bottom teeth)

should not conflict with the guidelines laid down by the respective Kennel Clubs, and when participating in competition whichever Standard and procedure is applicable should be complied with.

NECK
The long neck of an Italian is one of the features that helps to complete the graceful elegance of the head carriage. An 'ewe-shaped' neck, which means a neck with an over-accentuated bulge in the adam's apple area, is undesirable.

FOREQUARTERS
The long fine legs of an IG must be straight with neat pasterns. I have noticed some dogs are very upright in the leg, and others slope back slightly and have a slight bend on the pastern. By this, I do not mean a weakness in this department, merely a slight tendency to be longer in the

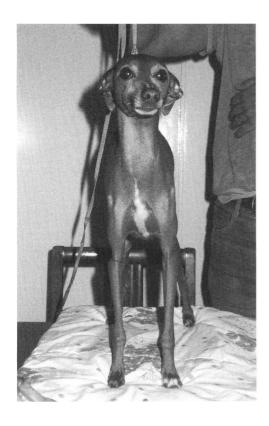

LEFT: Correct: good front showing depth of chest.

BELOW: Incorrect: all three Italians have bad fronts (and incorrect ear carriage). The dog pictured centre is 'out at elbows'.

pastern as opposed to a very upright pastern. Some believe the longer pastern means a stronger leg, but we have no veterinary proof of this. The shape of the front end as a whole is governed by shoulder placement.

HINDQUARTERS

There must be sufficient muscling to give the back legs the strength to propel them forward as required under the stipulations for gait and movement. When standing at the rear of the dog the judge should see both back legs standing equally balanced, turning neither in nor out. The curves of the stifles and thigh angulation, combined with the body shape, create the profile that is so admired in the breed. An Italian Greyhound that is required for exhibition must have sufficient muscle to give that nice rounded appearance over the thighs, but not the hard look of the rear end of a working dog. The aim is to achieve a happy medium.

Correct hindquarters with tail carried through.

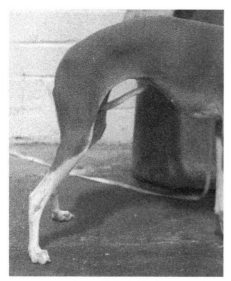

Note how the white markings can mislead.

Incorrect: too thin. The Italian should be well covered with the pin bone just visible.

BODY

The chest should be deep, but there should not be too much width between the two front legs when viewed from the front. There must be sufficient depth to allow for heart room, and yet the chest must not be so narrow as to give the impression that both legs have 'come out of the same hole' – an expression novice owners may hear from others.

The amount of weight the dog is carrying undoubtedly makes or mars the view of the body. A very skinny dog loses weight from all over, not just the belly area, and this includes the area of the anatomy just described. An IG should be sufficiently covered to allow just a suggestion of the hip bones to be seen through the skin. A very fat dog appears shorter on its front legs than it really is, and it also looks flat in topline. Owners will find that an IG who is over-indulged in the kitchen will appear 'loaded on the shoulders', i.e. it will have a top-heavy appearance.

The ribcage should be well-sprung; the chest that is short fails to give a nice rounded finish, instead it goes to rather more of a point over the keel, which is to be penalised. There are varying degrees of this particular problem, but it does exist. This will not change or 'improve' as a puppy matures.

The backline or 'topline', is an important feature. When the Italian is moving it should keep the desired curve over the loin. Many IGs stand perfectly well and, of course, they can be 'arranged' when being stacked by their handler, but on the move the dog is in control and it is surprising how different they can appear when you view a number together. I believe the interpretation in some of the European countries is that the outline should be more like the Sloughi with a flatter topline.

The back end of the dog should droop at the hindquarters, but not so far as to be extended like the rear end of a Whippet. Where the loin begins is the highest point of the curve of the back and these features combine to form a most definite tuck up at the flanks. If a dog is too fat, the tuck up nearly disappears, and if a dog is too thin, it roaches its back and appears to have no expanse of loin at all. When an Italian Greyhound is being presented it should not be stacked like a Whippet with the back feet placed well back over the ground; it should stand much more on a square.

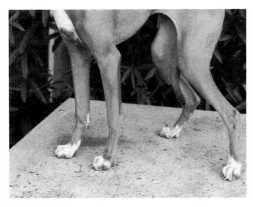

Correct: hare feet.

Incorrect: cat feet.

FEET
Many owners overlook the shape of their dog's feet, just taking them for granted. However, there is a distinct difference between the desired hare feet and the cat-shaped feet that are often seen. The nails should be kept trimmed so as to enhance the shape of the feet. Strangely enough, for all their elegance, an Italian Greyhound can actually seem to 'stamp' their feet when trying to get attention to go through a doorway or similar. It seems to fidget about on the spot and you wonder how such a dainty animal can patter so!

TAIL
The tail carriage is the final finishing-off of the body shape and balances the rest of the outline. Many hound judges gently hold the tail and see if it will reach down to the hock as this is the ideal length. The root of the tail should be set low, and sometimes the dog may have a reasonable length of tail but it appears shorter because it is set higher than desirable. A curly pig-shaped tail carriage is quite offensive to the eye and should be penalised heavily. A tail that is carried upwards is not the epitome of elegance either, but judges must decide whether this is a natural carriage or just high spirits because the dog is unsettled through being rushed into the ring. Sometimes in very hot weather a dog will hold its tail away from its rear end, as if this cools them. The tapered, long whip tail is the ideal, set on low.

COAT AND COLOUR
All colours should have the lovely soft and supple skin that you can actually lift gently with your fingers without pinching and hurting the dog. The actual hair must be short and the denser the

The range of colours (left to right): solid, pied and Irish. The FCI only permits solid-colours in its Breed Standard.

better. Here, some dogs do vary depending on their colour and breeding lines. The more coat per square inch the better, and this again is governed by genetic computation. The less dense the hair then the more the tendency for thinner patches during the winter months, at times of stress or in later years. In the main the fawns and blues seem to be the likeliest candidates for this problem.

If you are lucky enough to breed or own an Italian of these colours that permanently keeps all its coat, it is worthwhile investigating the pedigree thoroughly and finding out as much as you can from more experienced owners and breeders to try and hang on to this valuable asset. In my experience the white and red coloured dogs seem to have less of a problem. The coat should be as glossy as satin and positively glow with good health.

The actual colours that are allowed vary according to the different Breed Standards. The FCI do not allow the flashy 'Irish' marked, nor 'pieds', nor other white trims that are allowed in the other Standards. I think this is really a pity as these colours are popular with some owners, and as they have always been available I cannot quite understand why there is such bias. The Italian Greyhounds in the countries governed by the FCI still produce these 'banned' colours in litters from time to time because they are part of the breed's heritage, and these pups either have to be found pet homes or they may be culled at birth. Some breeders and owners hang on to these dogs in the hope that the ruling may one day be altered, but only time will tell whether there will be a change of heart – I certainly hope there will be.

Breeders have to consider the question of colour all the time when planning imports, for instance, and aim for only solid coloured lines. A few white hairs on the chest or toes is the only white allowed, plus a very few hairs on the tip of the tail. This particular distinction often occurs in Italians everywhere. Sometimes judges will allow a little white over the feet too, but to exhibit at the highest level the dog must be whole coloured.

GAIT/MOVEMENT

The size and the movement of the Italian Greyhound are the least compatible areas of the breed between the various countries. Judges and exhibitors often find it difficult to agree on the matter, but that is what makes it all the more interesting. In the USA , Canada, UK, Australia, and others

Different types of movement

Ch. Dairylane Savoir-Faire after winning his first CC at seven months. Note the correct lift and bend in the foreleg.

Am. Ch. Nelshire Jack of Diamonds, imported to Britain from the United States by Dr and Mrs D. Smith, BOB Crufts 1981.

Ch. Florita Favolosa, 27CCs and 15 RCCs. Became Breed Record Holder in May 1996. Owned by Miss Helen Lister. A good example of propulsion from the rear, in profile.

not conforming to the FCI Breed Standard, the action required is 'high stepping and free'.

Although there have been many arguments as to whether this is the same as 'hackney' movement as described in canine literature and comparisons made to the hackney action of some horses, we are not in this instance going to debate the point. The word 'hackney' is *not* contained in the Breed Standards so it should not be considered relevant, and I have never seen this point made in all the argument that has gone on over the years questioning its use. Some breeds include this adjective in their Breed Standards, so we must assume that the breeders who formulated it felt it appropriate.

Prior to 1985 the FCI Breed Standard in Italy had the word "saltellante" under the heading for movement. This, I understand from Gilberto Grandi, means "skipping or tripping" in the English language. This was changed because it was felt it was being misinterpreted to mean, in Gilberto's words, "an egg beating movement". In 1985 the FCI Standard was changed to read: "Elastica ed armonica" in Italian, "Elastique et harmonieuse" in French. Signor Grandi tells me this means "springy and harmonic". This is, in fact, just what the British and American Breed Standards require. We also want to see the Italian Greyhound covering the ground well – the forelegs reaching up and forward, to cover maximum area, and the hind legs moving with drive. We do *not* require short 'mincing' steps.

Obviously a smaller dog will cover less ground than a larger one, the area will naturally be governed by the size of the dog and therefore length of limbs. A good moving Italian Greyhound moving around a large ring, flows, and is the prettiest of sights. The addition of the comparison of the Italian Greyhound to a Sloughi as well as that to the Greyhound, which is included in the other Standards, does not seem to me to be beneficial. Surely the Italian Greyhound is a breed all on its own. Why do we compare it with anything? However the UK and USA Standards also include the comparison with the Greyhound.

My interpretation of the Breed Standard is that, when moving, the Italian should lift its front legs well off the ground with a slight bend in the knee, but it should still be able to reach forward and cover the ground in fairly large steps, not in a mincing manner. The knee should not come up so high as to appear to be under the chin. This is an absolutely different movement to the daisy-cutting action required in the Whippet, which is low over the ground.

At the same time the hind legs should move in a straight line following the front legs, without either of the back legs turning in or out. If a judge refers to a dog as 'pacing', this means that the two legs on the same side of the body are moving at the same time. A dog moving correctly should have the left front leg forward and the left hind leg back, and the right front leg back and the right hind leg forward. Those owners in countries governed by the FCI will know that 'high stepping' is considered a fault in their Breed Standard.

SIZE
Again, there is a difference in the Standards when it comes to the correct size for an Italian Greyhound, and breeders, exhibitors and judges must be guided by the appropriate ruling. The ideal is generally approximately 13-15 inches at the withers, or 38 cm (FCI), or 6-10 lbs weight. Unless scales and measuring hoops are used in the show ring, as in some breeds, the judge has to use his discretion and experience to know whether an exhibit is the correct size. Owners would do well to weigh and measure their dogs from time to time to keep themselves within the guidelines as much as possible. It is very easy to suffer from the delusion that all your stock is correct, and everyone else has the wrong-sized dogs, particularly if your dogs are uniform in size.

It also makes a difference when seeing different sized exhibits in different environments. It is hard to believe how much smaller a fairly tall exhibit can look when it is at an outdoor show. A tall exhibit that is standing next to a much smaller one, can give the impression that its neighbour is under-sized when it may be of the correct proportions. This also applies in reverse, of course. The eye can certainly play tricks in this regard as it can with colour and markings. Long white front legs can confuse the judge, who may get the impression the dog is taller that it actually is when looking at the front assembly. A splash of white marking across the chest area may make the dog appear to be wider than it is; a flash of colour across the shoulders may distort the picture and a dog with one white leg and one half-coloured leg will need a second glance.

When assessing any Italian Greyhound as a show specimen, I cannot stress enough that it is the whole dog that must be considered. It is no use if a judge places the smallest dog in the class in the first prize position if it is unsound, or has a small round head, a bad front, or any other outstanding fault. The priorities must always be the 'typical' look of the breed, and the dog must be able to move well and be thoroughly sound. Naturally, each judge will find some faults more horrendous in their eyes than others; if they did not, then the results at the shows would be extremely boring. We all hate some faults more than others. However, a judge should not fall into the trap of 'fault' judging, i.e. deliberately looking for a fault that they abhor and then placing the dogs in order on that basis. The dog as a whole is important; the grace and general beauty are paramount. It must *look* like an Italian Greyhound.

From an exhibitor's point of view, too, I would ask judges to allow plenty of time for their exhibits to move around the ring (within the time available) and then allow their handlers to restack their charges. Italian Greyhounds standing still for long periods do not show off to their best advantage and this makes the judge's task much harder. A dog can appear to fold up and really spoil the picture. As I have already stated, IGs do not always react well if they are over-handled by judges, and as all their faults and beauty spots are clearly visible to the eye, this should not really be necessary.

The trembling of the limbs that is often seen in Italian Greyhounds should not be considered a fault of temperament; while they should be able to stand their ground, this habit is commonplace. It does not always indicate they are feeling chilled either, although, of course, they will shiver in cold conditions. It is just an affectation that IGs seem to have, almost as if rippling their skin and muscles is a comfort to them. After all, it must be fairly boring to stand about waiting for us humans to decide which colour ribbon they should have! But some judges, who are not used to handling the breed, comment on this habit in a rather disparaging way, when it should be regarded as just another endearing characteristic of this lovely breed.

Chapter Six

WHITE MARKINGS ON THE ITALIAN GREYHOUND

For most breeders the colours of their puppies is secondary in importance to the construction. However, those following the FCI ruling obviously have to do their best to eliminate the chances of white appearing in their stock. Some kennels are associated with particular colours, solid or otherwise, because of their breeding programme. In my own programme I introduced a pied bitch, sired by my own stud dog, with the view that she was a pretty little soul, and she might introduce some white into my solid fawn litters. She went on to produce her four puppies, and all were all solid fawn! Yet my solid fawn bitch produced fawn with white trim (Irish marked) and a blue in another litter. Most of us have some idea as to what we *may* expect, depending upon the stud dog we use. Ruth Bloore (recently deceased) of the well-known Wavecrest kennels in the Santa Monica, California, USA, has researched the subject more thoroughly, however, and she offers the following advice for those who would really like to plan this aspect of breeding.

"Dr Clarence C. Little has explained the genetic inheritance of the 'White-Spotting' gene quite thoroughly in his book, *The Inheritance of Coat Color in the Dog*. It is considered that each of the genes assort independently and this is just one of the many genes that Dr Little has explained in coat color. In many loci, there are but two alleles: a simple Dominant and a simple recessive. This could be illustrated by the color genes which are a basic two: Black (B) which is Dominant and brown (b) which is recessive. Another illustration would be the depth of pigmentation locus: Deep pigmentation (D) which is Dominant and dilute pigmentation (d) which is recessive. However, in the White-Spotting locus, there are four separate alleles which can be listed like a step-ladder, with the Dominant on the top rung of the ladder and the next three in steps below, in order of their dominance.

"The top of the ladder is Solid (S) no white markings. Next in line is the Irish-spotted (s^i). These are dogs which are white in any or all of the areas which may include white feet, white legs, white collar, blaze, tail tip, white on throat or chest, etc. On the third rung down the ladder in sequence of dominance are pieds (s^P), which are white dogs with colored patches or spots of color. At the very bottom of the ladder is the pure white dog, or extreme white piebald (S^w). In

S: Solid.

S^i: Irish-spotted.

s^P: Piebald.

s^w: Extreme white piebald.

Italian Greyhounds the first three alleles are the ones most often encountered. This is the ladder: S—Solid (Self – or completely pigmented body surface), s^i – Irish spotting with few and definitely located white areas, s^P – piebald spotting, s^w – extreme white piebald. If we study this ladder we will see that S is dominant over all, that Irish spotting is dominant over pied and white, but it is recessive to Solid. Pied is recessive to both Solid and Irish spotting, but is dominant over white. And so it goes.

"Every dog is made up of pairs of genes. The sire provides one of its pair of genes in the sperm and the dam provides one of its pair of genes in the ovum. When these single genes unite in the fertilized egg, a new animal is conceived. The inherited gene that is Dominant will exhibit itself in the appearance of the animal. This is called his phenotype (the picture he presents). His genotype is his genetic formula, which includes both genes, one of which may be dominated or hidden by the other. Or it could possibly be that his pair of genes are identical, and he could have inherited the very same white spotting factor from each parent.

"Our Wavecrest Sweet William was a solid, self-colored fawn. He was bred to solid females, to Irish spotted females, to pied females. Every single puppy he sired was Solid. Some were solid fawn, some solid blue (if the dam were blue), some golden, some bronze, but every puppy was self-colored. From this we know that both of William's white spotting genes were Solid. His puppies' phenotype was solid, but their genotype was solid plus whatever white spotting gene the dam provided.

"We are able to look at an Italian Greyhound and say that it is self-colored, Irish spotted, pied or white, but usually one must test-breed to determine its whole genetic white-spotting formula. Occasionally, one single litter will tell the whole story. Our Ch. Wavecrest Golden Goddess is a fawn with white feet in front and a white chest pitch. We were not sure if she was an Irish spotted with very little white, or a solid with a bit of white.

"Our Ch. Roadrunner is the classic Irish spotted. He has four white stockings, complete white collar and shawl, white blaze and tail tip. The first mating between this pair revealed the whole story in the proper Mendelian ratio! There were two Solids, one Irish spotted and one pied. Roadrunner could not possibly carry a solid gene, because if he did, he would *be* a solid as it is dominant over all. So this established the fact that Goddess was a solid with pseudo Irish spotting. Now, the Irish spotted puppy had to have received from Goddess another white spotting allele other than her Solid gene. So we knew that Goddess carried one white spotting gene recessive to her solid. Now to the pied puppy. It couldn't have inherited either white spotting allele that was evident in its parents – Solid or Irish spotted. So the pied puppy revealed that the recessive hidden genes in its parents had to be pied.

"We can identify the sire as $s^i s^P$: Irish spotted with a pied recessive. We can identify the dam as Ss^P: Solid with a pied recessive. So, we are able to identify the white spotting factor on the four puppies as:
1. Solid, with a recessive Irish spotted gene – Ss^i.
2. Solid, with a recessive pied gene – Ss^P.
 3. Irish spotted, with a recessive pied gene – $s^i s^P$.
 4. Pied – $s^P s^P$.

"It is seldom that one first litter will tell the whole story, such as this one, and it might take many litters before all combinations could become apparent. What a delight it is to have Italian Greyhounds where we can have complete leeway in all colors and markings!

Chapter Seven

THE ITALIAN GREYHOUND IN BRITAIN

In 1851 the Great Exhibition was opened by Queen Victoria and Prince Albert at Crystal Palace, and this heralded the start of a new era for staging exhibitions. The gradual development of the railway made travelling much easier, and this was to have a major effect on every aspect of life in Victorian England. In 1859 the first organised dog show, which was for Pointers and Setters, took place at the Town Hall, Newcastle upon Tyne on the 28th and 29th of June. Other shows followed, and the Crystal Palace Show was first staged in 1870. After the second show at this venue Mr S. E. Shirley assembled a gathering of several gentlemen, who formed the Kennel Club. Within a short space of time the Stud Book was printed, which recorded wins at shows, dogs and their breeding.

At this time Italian Greyhounds were at a low point in the UK, mostly due to the desire for very tiny specimens. Fortunately, however, there were some breeders and owners involved who had the good of the breed at heart. By guaranteeing classes and specials for the breed they encouraged owners to breed for specific points and this encouraged competition. The Kennel Club introduced affixes for breeders in 1886, but not all owners adopted this procedure, and this can make the business of researching pedigrees far more complicated.

THE EARLY BREEDERS
Neither Miss Mackenzie (1836-1909) nor Mrs Scarlett (1851-1934) used affixes, and their Italians were known simply by names such as Dido, Juno, Saltarello, Solera and Sola. The well known show dogs belonging to Mr MacDonald during the 1870s were called Molly and Duke etc. In fact, Molly, who was born in 1866, was a well known winner for several years until her owner's death, and then she appears with another owner, namely Mrs Briggs. The bitch was now called Venus, and wins are recorded at the Crystal Palace, Brighton, Burton on Trent, and Hamburg in 1876. This would have made her quite an old exhibit, but it is clear that Molly and Venus were one and the same. Little importance was attached to changing a dog's name, and owners often had the same name for several dogs, and so considerable patience is required when trying to trace breed history. Quarantine did not become law until 1898, and this allowed a dog called Flip, who had been born in 1871 and imported from Spain, to be shown in Birmingham in 1875,

where he won first prize. The scarcity of IGs in the UK made breeding good specimens a problem. In 1874 forty were registered with the Kennel Club, but in 1875 only two were registered, and just four in 1876. Miss Mackenzie brought her original dogs with her from Italy, where she had lived for many years. Although these were larger than some already in the UK, she did not cross-breed them with any of the small terriers, as had been done by some breeders, and even though her show dogs gradually became smaller, no doubt because of the small gene pool available, they kept their quality and were sound and healthy. I gather the lady was quite an extrovert personality, and was well known around the dog shows, always wearing her poke bonnet and carrying her gamp umbrella. We are told that she preferred the fawn colour in her IGs. Much credit is due to this lady for her stalwart support of the breed until her death. Her other passion was apparently the music of Handel and she was a regular participant in the annual Handel Festival.

There were also the well known Italian Greyhounds belonging to Mr Anstice kept around 1887. They did win prizes in the late 1880s, but were not often shown. Mrs Cottrell-Dormer of the Rousham prefix and her friend Baroness Campbell Von Laurentz of the Rosemead prefix, bred quite a number of IGs. The Baroness's husband was aide de camp to Duke Ernest II, brother of the Prince Consort. The Baroness was very involved in running the breed club, but she relinquished her post as president in order to participate more in the exhibition of her dogs. Messrs Brown, Cliffe, Charlwood and Matthews were also keen fanciers of the period with regularly winning stock.

THE FIRST WORLD WAR
The First World War (1914-1918) took its toll on the breed. Some owners could not afford to keep their dogs and these were painlessly put to sleep with chloroform. This must have been a most unpleasant task, and all those who love their animals are grateful that the advanced anaesthetics of the nineties are far kinder. The precious Breeding Licences, brought into being by the Government of the day, were only rarely allocated and the financial aspect of rearing a litter also restricted breeding. Only a few of the old lines were left, and unfortunately some of these were rather large IGs, some also suffering from the effects of bad feeding during the War.

Mrs Scarlett writes very poignantly at this time, concerning the gift of a dog called Salvato – the last dog left of a kennel belonging to Mrs Brown. She writes: "Fawn, light, sunlight markings and 8½lbs, if as much, last dog of the kennel, never shown – War time – kennel done for – only Nancy left alive, Mr Brown died." This unregistered dog was "sent badly packed in a basket by a motor carrier and in a wild state of fright, had a fit and got away a whole week in the meadows. I got him back catching him just like a wild animal and got him perfectly well and very clever. Such a good companion, I could teach him anything." Apparently he sired a litter of puppies for a titled gentleman, but the dam overlaid them, much to the distress of Mrs Scarlett. She often refers to 'sunlight markings'. I presume this refers to the lighter colour often found around the shoulders on Italians.

Mrs Scarlett bought a puppy for ten guineas from Mrs C. Whale. The bitch was a little on the large side, but good quality. Unfortunately she was never bred from because she was stone deaf, and she fell ill and died before she was a year old. Mrs Whale then gave Mrs Scarlett the litter brother to care for, as he was also ill with some fading disease, like his sister. Despite much care, he too died. It seems a number of poultry were kept at the premises of the breeder, and dogs and chickens all used the same small area of ground, so they wondered if infection had been

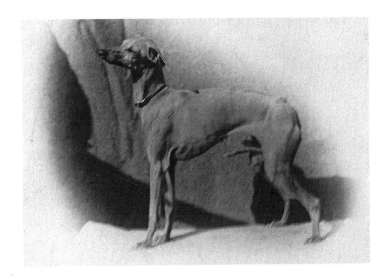

Isola Daphne: imported USA 1926.

introduced to the dogs via the soiled ground. Mrs Scarlett's bad luck continued, for the next IG she purchased was a black bitch called Sarascina. She was imported from Paris, and then broke her leg in quarantine. At the same time Miss Porter of the Isola prefix acquired the litter sister, who was blue. Unfortunately she had prick ears, but both were considered to be of quality. However, another disaster struck when Sarascina died of fits before being bred from. Curiously, her litter sister died at almost the same time, suffering a fit when a Fox Terrier jumped out of a hedge at her while she was being exercised by her owner on the Isle of Wight.

There were one or two IGs with bloodlines back to Adolphus (called 'Dolphy' in some pedigrees and records). He had been brought to London from Italy by the Misses (Signorinas) Bartilozzi in the late 1880s, and was owned by Miss Gillatt. He was bred from the family's long line of Italians. It seems they had a number of the breed all between 6lbs and 12lbs in weight. He was fawn and white, and his sire was fawn with a lot of white. Two sons remained, Punchinello and Boyo, both sons of Juno who was a 'Jack' daughter bred by Miss Mackenzie.

THE TWENTIES AND THIRTIES
Miss E. D. Gilpin, later Mrs E. D. Thring, had become interested in IGs in the mid 1920s, and her Pinea prefix was to become well known. Pinea Perlette, born in 1924, was given to Mrs Scarlett. Mrs Thring took over as secretary of the breed club from Mrs Scarlett in 1928 and continued in office until 1960 – a pair of very dedicated ladies. Miss Porter imported Isola Daphne and Isola Princess from the Aira Vana Kennel in Indiana, USA. Daphne was bred by Mrs M. P. Norton, born on March 12th 1923, sire Colonels Laddie, dam Roma II. Princess was born on March 29th 1926, sired by Dinty Dee out of Imogene. It seemed that this American strain had been alive for forty years or more.

Litters of seven or eight puppies were very common at this time, and those that were pure-bred were all of one type, varying in size only. Some were naturally better than others. There were defects such as faulty ears, or tails, or being too heavy in bone, but they were of good Italian 'type'. Mrs Mills had a well known brood bitch called 'Myra', who was too big for show but she produced several winning offspring. Miss Porter (Isola) kept around fifteen IGs on the Isle of Wight, and apparently they were all beautifully matched; Mrs Thring had around twenty IGs at one time. Earlier there had been some good IGs in Hamburg, Germany, belonging to Herr Doorst, but in 1924 his grandson imported two dogs from Mrs Thring's kennel as by then there were so few good pure-breds to be found in his own country.

As one generation overlaps another, so newer names appear. Some breeders seem to have produced lots of litters over a concentrated span of time, and then they disappear from the records. Imports continued and the Springinsfeld affix appears on dogs from Austria. Evidently Frau Pfleger founded this kennel of IGs in approximately 1930. Some of her dogs were a little large in the early stages, but she worked hard to reduce this while still producing sound, good Italians. She acquired a dog from Count Cavillino in Italy in 1935. In 1936 Mrs Mills imported Robbart Springinsfeld (Xitto Springinsfeld – Utta Springinsfeld), born December 1st 1935, and in 1937 Mrs E. Horner brought over another male, Percy Springinsfeld, born June 3rd 1936. His sire was also Xitto (gs Claus vd Ostee, gd Zierde Springinsfeld) and his dam was Zarte Springinsfield (gs Rittertsportn v Westerberg, gd Gelge vd Ostee).

The Second World War interrupted the lives of owners and breeders once again, and more restrictions on the breeding of dogs came into force.

THE POST-WAR PERIOD

In 1949 Mrs Massey Cooke (Velletri) and her daughter Cynthia Howard (Ashgreen), whose interest in Italians had begun during the 1930s, brought over Brucemiks Sam from America. Although Sam was to prove an important influence, he was only used at stud for a short time as he was infected with hardpad which consequently made him sterile. These days we take all the the immunisation programmes for granted, but at this time it was very common to see dogs advertised for sale or at stud as being 'over distemper'. A couple of years later Mrs Massey Cooke and Mrs Howard imported Agnesina Savelli from Frau Baronin von Woyrsch from Germany.

Championship shows in the UK were suspended in September 1939 and recommenced May 1946 when hostilities had ceased. Charles Cruft, who organised the first Dog Show of this name in 1891, died in 1938, and in 1948 this show was taken over by the Kennel Club. In 1924 the Kennel Club had decided that if, in any year ending December 3lst, there had been fewer than twenty registrations in a breed, that breed should not be entitled to Challenge Certificates during the following year. Consequently it was not until 1955 that Italian Greyhounds were once again able to regain this status.

At the Crufts Show in 1955 there was an entry of twelve dogs making eighteen entries, and they were judged by Mr W. Macdonald Daly. He wrote about Golden Arrow, the bitch CC winner, who became the first post-war bitch Champion: "A long way the best here, with her high-stepped typical action, elegant outlook and outline, nice fine coat." The dog CC winner was Mrs H. Y. Mansfield's Dudolino Of Velletri. The judge wrote: "Won comfortably on his outlook, type and quality, though inclined at times to go a bit oddly behind." Mrs Massey Cooke and Mrs Howard must have been delighted, as Golden Arrow was a daughter of Agnesina Savelli and sired by a son of Sam, as was Dudolino, who became the first male Champion. The litter sister to Golden Arrow, Grisell of Velletri was to prove invaluable in South Africa.

Mrs M. Barnard, a bulldog breeder, bred and owned many Italians who had great influenece in

Philtre Gigi Angilita: foundation of Mrs R. Lewis's Philtre kennel.

the longterm. Serenade of Silvershowers, born 1953, was her foundation bitch (Polo of Goblingreen – Bianca of Oldetimes). Polo and Bianca were both sired by Brucemiks Sam. Mrs Barnard purchased Noways Editie Clocke V. Damiate from Holland and the Canadian Champion bitch, Palermo Twinkling Star, from Mr Gilbert, and used them to advantage in her breeding programme.

The bitch arrived in whelp to Can. Ch. Bambi Boy of Palermo. She whelped in quarantine, producing two bitches and one dog, and although Mrs Barnard was able to bring the puppies out at six weeks of age, the dam had to remain in kennels for the remainder of her term. Twinkling Star was not exhibited in the UK, but her son, Noways Starlight, was Reserve CC winner at Crufts 1955 to Dudoline.

Mr and Mrs D. Morgan purchased the litter sister to Serenade, and the impact of the Nagrom Italian Greyhounds was soon felt. These kennels were also responsible for several imports, particularly from Italy, including the bitch Nagrom Borina Di Salabo (Nemo Di Salabo – Isotta Di Solcio), born on April 27th 1954, bred by Contessa davico Di Quittengo, and the male, Nagrom Gypsy Di San Siro (Earl v. Bayerischen Meer, Int.Ch. – Etna Di San Siro. Ch.), born in 1954, bred by Irmgard Bianchi-Muller. Progeny from these imports were not only exhibited in the UK, but also sent to other countries. Black and blue Italians were quite dominant among the Nagrom dogs.

It was because of Golden Arrow that Mrs M. B. Garrish, already well respected with her Whippet kennel, became besotted with the breed. In 1956 Mrs Garrish and Mrs Rieley, owner of Golden Arrow, were invited to the television studios to appear on a programme about Crufts. Mrs Garrish came with some Whippet pups, Mrs Rieley brought Golden Arrow, and Judy de Casembroot (who died in 1992) came with her Crufts Best in Show Greyhound, Treetops Golden Falcon.

Apparently, Mrs Garrish was so entranced with the temperament of the Italian Greyhound that

Ch. Fleeting Chichele Atalanta: foundation of Mrs M. B. Garrish's Fleeting line.

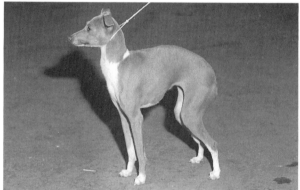

Ch. Noways Matthew, who figures on many pedigrees all over the world.

Ch. Noways Rosina (a daughter of Ch. Noways Matthew): Best in Show at the first IG club show in 1961. Bred and owned by Mrs M. Barnard.

she booked a puppy, although a litter was not imminent. A puppy arrived sooner rather than later, because Golden Arrow and Chichele Assam Carlo (bred by Mlle Y. Chardon and imported from France by Mrs Rieley) took matters into their own hands! Two bitches and one dog were born, and Mrs Garrish chose a blue with white trimmed bitch to be known as Ch. Fleeting Chichele Atalanta. This started a line of some eighteen Champions with many winners exported overseas.

Many pedigrees of today contain the Berinshill prefix belonging to Diana Waugh, who actually lived in America for a while. Her kennel began to include Italians, and Noways Pandora of Chelstoncross, also by Bambi Boy out of Can. Ch. Juliette of Palermo passed into her ownership. Imports included Am. Ch. Harbridge Royal Reward. The Estradas, owned by Messrs Scholes and Street, was another kennel of note at this time, as pedigrees reveal, and a number of imports were made by Mr Samuelson, Mrs Horsfall and Mrs Rieley, from Canada, Austria and Italy. Ulisse di Peltrengo Of Winterlea was purchased from Marchesa Montecuccoli in 1956 by Mrs M. Mooney, a Chihuahua breeder. The Italian breeding of Ulisse was very influential in the UK as he sired Ch. Noways Matthew (bred by Mrs M. Barnard) who is on so many of the pedigrees. Ulisse was then sent to America. In fact, more than one import came from the Marchesa to the Winterlea kennel.

In 1958 Rae Lewis's Philtre kennel came on the scene with a bitch to be known as Philtre Gigi Angilita. In possession of £25 that had been given her as a birthday present by her husband, she answered an advertisement in the paper for an IG. She previously kept Poodles, and some other breeds. Angilita was sired by Chichele Assam Carlo – Honeygaze Primavera. She was eventually mated to Mrs Garrish's Fleeting Noways Antonio – and the rest is history! Many Champions have followed, and four different Philtre Champion bitches have won Toy Groups. So many breeders have cause to be grateful for a Philtre bitch for the start of a successful kennel – myself included in 1972.

THE SIXTIES

The number of IGs registered at the Kennel Club in 1961 was 161, a figure which has never been reached since. To enlarge the gene pool Mrs Garrish and Mrs Barnard (Fleeting and Noways) imported Ch. Odin Springinsfeld, born in April 1964, from Austria in 1966 from Mrs P. Pfleger (Drottningberget's Firlefanz – Koralle Springinsfeld) and he soon became an English Champion and was to have a tremendous influence on the breed.

His son, Ch. Fleeting Flavius, bred by Mrs Garrish, was the Breed Record Holder until 1996 with twenty-three Challenge Certificates – and CCs were available at fewer shows then, compared with now. The nearest rival to Flavius's record was Mrs Palmer's (formerly Carter) Ch. Atina Satchmo with twenty-one CCs to his credit. Satchmo is solid fawn, born April 23rd 1983, sired by Ch. Atina Trista out of Atina Tali. Behind the Atinas are the Philtre dogs belonging to Mrs Lewis, and he also has a line back to Odin.

The Larchwoods, Pequas, Hobbitshills, Sheumacs, Smileyknowes, all contributed to the breed in the sixties and were responsible for once again bringing the breed to public attention. It was in 1964 that the first major win for the breed amongst competition with other breeds was achieved. Betty Samuels was already a keen Dachshund exhibitor, and at the Manchester Championship Show in 1963, Mrs E. A. Sandland, a breeder of Dachshunds and Italians, told her of a nice puppy she had at home which she thought she might sell. On returning home Mrs Samuels decided she would see the puppy, and eventually she purchased the little bitch, aged six and a

Ch. Sheumac Silvertips with Mrs Betty Samuels (left), and Ch. Fleeting Fangio with Mrs M.B. Garrish (right), 1964.

Ch. Fleeting Fine 'n Dandy (black) 1976. (Fleeting Furore – Nagrom Teresa).

Garwood.

half months. The cost was £25 and another £5 was to be paid if she was 'made up'. She became Ch. Sheumac Silvertips. Her sire was Sucops Fleeting Fiat and her dam was Nagrom Perla. She was born on August 3lst, 1962 and her pedigree meant that she had, through her sire, a line back to Ulisse, Primo, and, through her dam, the Italian and American dogs Ch. Nagrom Gypsy Di San Siro and Brucemiks Sam.

Her place in the history books of Italian Greyhounds was assured when she won her fifth Challenge Certificate and Best of Breed from Mrs M. Barnard at the Three Counties Championship Show in 1964. The Toys were held on the third day of the show, June 18th 1964, and the other Groups were Hounds and Terriers. She won the Best Toy award and then Best of the three Groups that day. The late Mr W. Siggers awarded overall Best in Show over the three days of the show to a Miniature Poodle. The next year at the WELKS Championship show in 1965 she again won Best of Breed from the late Mr L. H. Glover; in fact in all she won eight

Ch. Tamoretta Tailormade: the only IG to win Best in Show over all days at a Championship show. (Tamoretta Tanzaro – Tamoretta Loving Gladness). Born April 9th, 1976, died October 20th, 1992.

BoB's with her tally of eleven CCs. At this show Mrs L. M. Daly also awarded her Best in Toy Group. The other Groups competing on this day were Hounds, Gundogs, and Poodles. Evidently the Poodles were not in the Utility Group then, as they are these days. Mrs Daly awarded her Reserve Best in Show on this First Day.

Nowadays all the Group winnners compete against each other on the *last* day of a Championship show. There are no individual *daily* Best in Show or Reserve Best in Show winners. Sadly, Mrs Samuels was never able to have puppies from this lovely bitch as Silvertips died in whelp at the very young age of four and a half years. However, she will not be forgotten by IG exhibitors.

THE SEVENTIES
Another influential arrival on the Italian Greyhound scene was in l973 when The Hon. Mrs A. Marshall (then Leigh) imported from her native Sweden Sobers Solo, bred by Mrs A. Jonnson (Swedish Ch. Sobers Ior – Sobers Evolina) and his litter sister Sobers Sorella, to join her Tamoretta kennel, founded in 1968. Solo's granddaughter, Ch. Tamoretta Tailormade, is still the only IG to win a Best in Show over *all* the days at a Championship Show in the UK. This was Windsor in 1976 under the late Mr H. Essam. During l976/8 she won six Toy Groups, including Crufts 1980 – a record that has yet to be beaten. Her father is also a Toy Group winner, and she has produced winning offspring including the super stud dog Ch. Tamoretta Tidalwave of Turigner. Quite a record all told. She lived to be sixteen years of age.

RECENT IMPORTS
More recently, most of the imports to the UK have been brought in by Dr and Mrs D. Smith (Narrabo) who have imported dogs from the USA and South Africa. In fact, they exported South African Ch. Canta Libre Quite Rightly of Bonne to Sweden in 1991, and he is sired by Narrabo Jumping Jouster. Jouster was bred by Dr and Mrs Smith and exported to Alison Parkhouse in South Africa. His dam, De La Tremouille Gloriana was imported by the Smiths from Mrs Miller in South Africa. These imports and that of Mrs P. Spencer (Rilloby) are beginning to prove their

Ch Patchwork of Dairylane: Best of Breed Crufts 1983, pictured in the Warwick Vase presented to the winner in breed. This first CC came from the late Mr Bobby James, and her litter brother, Ch. Rearsbylea Adonis of Ishkoodah, owned by Mrs L. Chapman and bred by Mrs J. Cox, won the dog CC. He was to win BoB in 1984. Their sire was Dairylane Pink Panther.

*Ch. Viebrin
Manolito.
Owned and bred
by Mrs V.
Cantrill, 1985.*

worth. Offspring have already shown that when carefully mated to the right partners in the UK they can only add to the quality of the dogs available. Other Italian Greyhounds in the late 1990s have also been imported from Alison by newer owner Mrs J. Amsel (Artmeis).

I think it is fair to conclude that the Italian Greyhound today is a very cosmopolitan animal, with all countries having a share of each other's bloodlines. The current breeders in the eighties and nineties, who probably began their kennels in the seventies, are all based on these older lines, and therefore the early imports too. Knowing how to mix the few families of dogs is the craft of the true Italian Greyhound breeder. Newer owners who may become breeders of Italians, sometimes have to learn the hard way what mixes and what does not. There is not a particularly high demand for the breed as pets, and therefore this discourages all of us from breeding too many litters.

THE JUDGING SYSTEM

For a dog to be given the title of Champion in the UK it has to win three separate Challenge Certificates from three different judges, and one of these must be given after twelve months of age. Exhibitors rarely enter twice under a judge who has already given their exhibit a CC, but Crufts is considered the exception to the rule. There are a range of classes from Puppy to Open at the Championship Shows and a CC can be awarded by the judge to the winner of any of these classes as he or she thinks fit. The Reserve in each sex receives the Reserve Challenge Certificate (RCC). Exhibits that are already Champions have to enter the Open class. The exhibitors can always enter their dogs in classes higher than they have qualified for, but not lower. This means that all the dogs who are hoping to become Champions have to compete against dogs that already have their titles.

Ch. Philtre Farima: Toy Group winner 1985, BoB Crufts 1986. (Hyjinx Bright Star – Ch. Philtre Flo-Ella). From a strong bitch line: ggm Ch. P. Florena, gm Ch. P. Florita. Flo-Ella is a litter sister to Philtre Fleur de Louis (behind the Fleetgrace kennel) and also dam of Ch. P. Foulla and Ch. P. Fiori. Fiori is the dam of Ch. Philtre Faroah for Jemalsheva, top IG in 1992, bred by Mrs R. Lewis, owned by Mrs H. Davis.

Three Counties Championship Show 1988. Mrs M. Sprague-White (left) and BoB winner Ch. Fleetgrace Simya who won the Toy Group that day, and judge Mrs J. Minns. The dog CC winner, Mrs S. Vincent's Ch. Chelanis Achilles, is pictured right.

After the classes for dogs and bitches are complete (each sex competes separately) the Dog and Bitch Challenge Certificate winners compete for Best of Breed. After the BoB judging these winners then compete in their respective groups, and in the case of the Italian Greyhound this means the Toy Group. Championship Shows are the only shows where the Kennel Club issue Challenge Certificates. The other lesser shows are Open, Limited and Sanction and it is at these other shows that judges, exhibitors and exhibits learn their craft.

A Challenge Certificate that is won at Crufts Dog Show is not worth any more than a Challenge Certificate won at any other Championship Show in the UK, whereas in some countries an award at their major show is worth sometimes double that of the same award elsewhere. However, there is always an extra thrill in winning at the kennel Club's premier show, with all the added media attention. Equally, it is considered a great honour to judge at Crufts. Entries at shows vary from year to year, with Club events always drawing larger

Ch. Shahaab of Atina (Atina Rossini – Rivasura Royal Classic), owned and handled by Y. Palmer. Bred by Mrs Carter and Mrs V. Ford, 1988. He sired Ch. Atina Ashaya (1989), Ch. Sandene High Flyer (1991) and Ch. Jemalsheva Isis (1991).

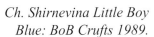

Ch. Shirnevina Little Boy Blue: BoB Crufts 1989.

numbers. Crufts usually attracts bigger entries, although exhibitors have to qualify their dogs in order to enter them. In Crufts Centenary year (1991) the total entry was sixty IGs, judged by Hon. Mrs A. Marshall (Tamoretta); BoB was Jon and Joan Hardcastle's Ch. Salspa Sapphire. In 1992 I had a lovely entry of fifty-seven dogs. My Best of Breed winner was a new owner and exhibitor, who had only been showing her dog for ten months! Berinshill Sophia had her first really big win that day. Sophia won her first CC and Best of Breed, and was a finalist in the Toy Group. Her young owner, Miss N. Hunter, certainly had a day to remember and Sophia became a Champion shortly afterwards.

GROUP WINNERS

It is rare for an Italian Greyhound to win a Toy Group. Some believe Italians are unfairly overlooked by the Toy Group judges, but it has to be said that a smooth-coated breed does have

Crufts 1992. BoB winner and Toy Group finalist Berinshill Sophia (left), now a Champion, owned by Miss N. Hunter. Pictured right, the dog CC winner, Mrs M. Sprague-White's Ch. Berinshill Azadah of Fleetgrace. Both were bred by Mrs C. A. Boyle and Mrs D. Waugh, and were the result of a repeat mating between Ch. Merry Monarch of Berinshill and Berinshill Shakia.

to have that extra razamatazz to attract the eye of the judge at this level. At an outdoor show, the elements can sometimes detract, particularly if a late afternoon breeze is blowing. However, more and more often Italians are being at least brought out into the last few, and sixteen in all have won the Toy Groups:– Firstly Ch. Sheumac Silvertips, then Mrs Lewis's Ch. Philtre Florena at Southern Counties in 1967, Ch. Tamoretta My Meridian at LKA in 1972, Mrs Lewis again with Ch. Philtre Florita, who is a daughter of Florena, at Blackpool in 1972; then my own Ch. Philtre Fayetta Of Dairylane at Three Counties in 1975; Mrs Marshall with all Tailormade's wins 1978/1980; Maureen Oliver's Ch. Sandene Altares at the Scottish Kennel Club Championship Show in 1981; Shirley Vincent's Ch. Chelanis Finest Kind at the Welsh Kennel Club Show in 1983; Mrs and Miss Turner's Ch. Turigner Blue Mermaid at the Scottish Kennel Club Championship Show in 1984; Mrs Y. Carter's (now Palmer) Ch. Atina Satchmo in 1985 at Blackpool; and unbelievably the same year Mrs Lewis with Ch. Philtre Farima at the South Wales K.A.; in 1988 Marian Sprague-White's Ch. Fleetgrace Simya at Three Counties Championship Show; Mrs Waugh and Mrs Boyle's Ch. Merry Monarch of Berinshill at Windsor in 1990; Mrs Helen Davis's Ch. Philtre Faroah of Jemalsheva at LKA 1992 (also Reserve Best in show); Mrs F.B. and Miss R. Turner's Ch. Turigner Wirlwind at South Wales Kennel Association in 1998; and Ch. Salatini Poeme, Three Counties Championship Show 2001.

INFLUENTIAL FAMILIES

Aust. and Eng. Ch. Odin Springinsfeld, imported by Mrs M. B. Garrish and Mrs M. Barnard, was the sire of Ch. Fleeting Flavius (the first breed CC record holder), Ch. Noways Fleeting Flaminia, Ch. Fleeting Floribunda and Ch. Fleeting Fenella of Follysend. Ch. Fleeting Flavius (dam: Fleeting Noways Flavius) was the father of Juneric Red Admiral and his litter sister Ch. Juneric Cleopatra, bred by Mr and Mrs E. Minns, out of Ch. Madam of the Meripak, born March 23rd 1968. Red Admiral did not gain his title (one CC and numerous Reserve CCs), as he invariably had to stand second to his famous sire. However, he was the sire of Ch. Philtre Florita (born August 8th 1969) out of Ch. Philtre Florena, plus Ch. Tentyra Senusret (born May 12th

Aust. & Eng. Ch. Odin Springinsfeld.

Ch. Fleeting Flavius. Breed CC record holder with 23 CCs until 1996 (see Ch. Florita Favolosa p.49).

Ch. Philtre Fleurette (Philtre Renaldo of Pequa – Ch. Philtre Florena). Foundation bitch of the Tentyra kennel.

*Ch. Nailati
Monarch Mylo of
Berinshill (Ch.
Tentyra Senusret
– Ch. Innocenza
of Traylane).*

*Dairylane Sweet
William (above) and
Dairylane Pink
Panther (left), (Ch.
Nailati Monarch
Mylo of Berinshill –
Ch. Philtre Fayetta
of Dairylane).*

1971) and his litter mate Ch. Tentyra Shalomith, bred by the late Mrs M. C. Fraser out of her foundation bitch Ch. Philtre Fleurette.

Ch. Philtre Fleurette was the mother of five Champions and was bred by Mrs Lewis. The other three were Ch. Tentyra Sekhmet, Mrs Vincent's Ch. Tentyra Caesarina and Mrs Castle's Ch. Tentyra Serket. Senusret's offspring included: Ch. Nailati Monarch Mylo of Berinshill (born December 26th 1972, winner of seventeen CCs), Ch. Philtre Fanina, Ch. Tamoretta Tidalwave of Turinger, Ch. Fenbeach Summer Sprite, Ch. Philtre Flo-Ella, and Ch. Hyjinx Sweet Sensation. Mylo was the father of Ch. Berinshill Panache, Ch. Tentyra Sekhmet, Ch. Tentyra Serket, Ch. Narrabo Sweet N' Neat (exported to South Africa), Ch. Parpico Blue Rose, Ch. Sandene Altares, Ch. Sandene Artaius (litter mates), and Ch. Tamoretta That's Talent.

When Mylo was mated to Ch. Philtre Fayetta of Dairylane they produced the litter mates

Sobers Solo. Imp. Sweden. (sire of Tamoretta Tanzaro asnd grandfather of Ch. Tamoretta Tailormade).

Ch. Tamoretta Tidalwave of Turigner (Ch. Tentyra Senusret – Ch. Tamoretta Tailormade).

Tamoretta Time After Time (Ch. Nailati Monarch Mylo of Berinshill – Ch. Tamoretta Tailormade).

Dairylane Pink Panther and Dairylane Sweet William. Neither gained their Championships. I considered Pink Panther to be up to size but very houndy; he had lovely movement, which was much admired by several eminent breeders of the day. He was not campaigned. Sweet William was small, very typy and won two CCs and seven Reserve CCs. Like Red Admiral he was often in contention with his sire in the ring. He then lost a front tooth and was withdrawn from the ring, perhaps, with hindsight, foolishly. However, although they were never used at stud extensively, they sired ten Champion children between them.

Dairylane Pink Panther was the father of Ch. Chelanis Enchantress, Ch. Rearsbylea Adonis, Ch. Patchwork of Dairylane, Ch. Narrabo Siskin of Myroak and Australian Ch. Narrabo Merely A Monarch. Dairylane Sweet William fathered Ch. Nadilee Red Chiffon of Berinshill, Ch. Chelanis Finest Kind, Ch. Chelanis Sassafras, Ch. Dairylane Savoir-Faire, and Ch. Jaswyn Sea Pearl. Siskin and Merely a Monarch were out of a daughter of the dog imported from the USA by Dr and Mrs D. Smith, Am. Ch. Nelshire's Jack of Diamonds. Siskin's daughter, owned and bred by Mrs J. Saunders, has also gained her title. She is Ch. Myroak Marcasite and was sired by S. Af. Ch. Quite Rightly of Bonne, exported to Sweden by Dr and Mrs Smith.

Tamoretta Time After Time, winner of one CC, is litter brother to Ch. Tamoretta That's Talent out of Ch. Tamoretta Tailormade. He is sire of Int. Ch. Dairylane Moody Blue, Ch. Shirnevina Little Boy Blue, Ch. Shirnevina Once Upon a Time, Ch. Shirnevina Wee Willie Winkie (all three Shirnevinas have a Tamoretta dam), and Ch. Favorita Favolosa. That's Talent sired Ch. Tamoretta Midnight Marauder of Viebrin and Ch. Parpico Rosetta. The pedigree lines go back to Ch. Golden Arrow of Velletri and Tulerone Berinshill Romulus, who has Chichele Assam Carlo as his sire and Noways Pandora of Chelstoncross as his dam, bringing together Springinsfeld breeding behind Assam Carlo and the Canadian kennel of Palermo behind Pandora.

Ch Tamoretta Tailormade was mated on the first occasion to Ch. Tentyra Senusret (sire of Mylo). This union produced Ch. Tamoretta Tidalwave of Turigner (born August 20th 1977) owned, loved and exhibited by the partnership of Mrs W. F. B. Turner and her daughter Rebecca Turner. Rupert, who is now a very elderly IG, has been of great influence. Combining all the lines already mentioned, he was also chosen by Pat Spencer on her return from South Africa to mate to her South African Ch. Rilloby Fig Leaf of Cante Libre producing the 1990 top winning IG, Ch. Rilloby One Man Band, who has also been used at stud. It is, however, a little premature to evaluate the outcome of his offspring. His litter sister is Ch. Rilloby Crackling Rosie of Salvo. Tidalwave has also sired Ch. Turigner Goldcrest, Ch. Turigner Blue Mermaid, Ch. Viebrin Manolito, Ch. Parpico Twice Brightly and Ch. Turigner Bluebutton at Mildorma.

Sobers Solo, imported from Sweden by the Hon. Mrs A. Marshall, is sired by Ch. Sobers Ior out of Sobers Evolina and is a great grandson of Int. & Nord. Ch. Quirina Del Calcione. There are several of the Italian Del Calcione names in his pedigree including Ch. Dik Dik Del Calcione, on both sides. Chichele Assam Carlo from France also appears, as well as several of the Nagrom dogs.

KENNEL CLUB REGISTRATIONS

[Reproduced by kind permission of the English Kennel Club]

Year	No	Year	No	Year	No	Year	No
1906	10	1930	11	1954	14	1977	68
1907	24	1931	13	1955	47	1978	124
1908	27	1932	21	1956	49	1979	144
1909	23	1933	24	1957	63	1980	152
1910	13	1934	07	1958	100	1981	133
1911	19	1935	20	1959	136	1982	111
1912	15	1936	21	1960	158	1983	114
1913	15	1937	29	1961	198	1984	90
1914	10	1938	16	1962	167	1985	78
1915	05	1939	23	1963	138	1986	86
1916	05	1940	02	1964	140	1987	63
1917	03	1941	11	1965	140	1988	60
1918	01	1942	04	1966	127	1989	97
1919	00	1943	05	1967	119	1990	82
1920	05	1944	05	1968	136	1991	88
1921	04	1945	05	1969	111	1992	89
1922	05	1946	14	1970	167	1993	117
1923	04	1947	09	1971	105	1994	121
1924	14	1948	13	1972	125	1995	101
1925	08	1949	11	1973	124	1996	90
1926	23	1950	09	1974	134	1997	133
1927	27	1951	10	1975	95	1998	128
1928	29	1952	05	1976	59	1999	121
1929	21	1953	34				

NB No accurate figures available 1900-1905.

Restrictions in place on breeding dogs during First World War 1914-1918 and Second World War 1939-1945. Towards the close of 1992, 147 IGs had been awarded their Championship title in Britain since the Second World War.

Chapter Eight

THE ITALIAN GREYHOUND IN NORTH AMERICA

THE SHOW SYSTEM

The system of awarding Championship titles is rather different in the USA and Canada from the UK, and the American and Canadian exhibitors often have to travel much longer distances to achieve this goal. Many own motor homes, and so they can take their whole IG family and enjoy the company of other IG fanciers by sharing picnics and barbeques together. Some exhibitors at the British shows 'caravan' or have a motor home too, but not in the same numbers. This mode of transport is particularly useful for the American 'circuits' or 'cluster' shows when two to four consecutive shows are held within the same area and sometimes on the same site. Again this is different from the British show scene, where each Championship Show is held at a different venue, some considerable distance apart.

In the USA there are three national Specialties each year, one in the East, one in the West and a third that 'roves'. These are considered by exhibitors the most worthwhile venues at which to compete with their Italian Greyhounds, as there are many good dogs and therefore good competition, which means a worthwhile assessment of your exhibits. At a recent East coast Specialty there were 170 entered and the winner was Ch. Tekoneva's Dario owned by Carol Harris and Sandra Katy. Some owners prefer to hand over the care of their dogs to professional handlers who will do the travelling for them, whereas one very rarely sees a professional handler in an IG ring in the UK. Fifteen points are required to enable an IG to become a Champion under the American Kennel Club Regulations system, and two of these must be Major points. They are also dependent upon the number of dogs entered at the shows.

In the same way that the Crufts Dog Show in the UK is considered by outsiders to be the highlight of the show season, in the United States it is the Westminster Kennel Club Show that holds the equivalent media attention. The American Kennel Club was not founded until 1884, but there were dog shows being held in the USA before this date. The Westminster Kennel Club show was one of the early successful shows in the USA, and it has held shows every year since 1877. The American Kennel Club Stud Book dates from 1878, thanks to Dr Rowe who gave his records to the AKC in 1889. Until June 1952 every dog was registered, but subsequently it has

Showground US style, Sir Francis Drake KC, Marin County, California.

been confined to dogs who have reproduced. In the UK all the Championship Shows have 'benching', i.e. cages placed on rows of benches, provided by the show organisers. The dogs should be kept in these for the majority of the proceedings, except for exercising them and while they are being judged. In the USA at the Westminster event, held in Madison Square Garden, New York, benching is provided and the above rules apply, but at their other Championship shows, it is not, and the dogs are only required to be present for the judging. In 1992 entries at Westminster were confined to Champions, although in the past there were few dogs entered that were not already Champions. Like Crufts, Westminster attracts many visitors and is seen as a showcase for the really top dogs who have been campaigned more seriously. Winning in the Groups must be a thrilling experience.

WINNERS AT WESTMINSTER
Larry and Audrey Sutton of the Westwind prefix have had their share of wins at Westminster with the incredible record of their fawn and white Am. and Can. Ch. Westwind's Sweet And Sassy, who was Best of Breed at Westminster in 1986, 1987 and 1988. Sassy retired at the end of February 1988 after winning her fiftieth Toy Group first. Her amazing show career included Best of Breed at a Canadian IG Specialty and Toy Group first at seven months; Best of Breed at four Italian Greyhound Club of American National Specialties and one regional IG Specialty; two all breed Best in Shows, plus being placed in the Toy Groups more times than being left out and

Am. & Can. Ch. Westwind's Sweet And Sassy: Best of Breed at Westminster in 1986, 1987 and 1988. Owned and bred by Larry and Audrey Sutton, handled by Donald Rodgers. Note how the lead is tightened sufficiently behind the ears to keep the bitch's head held high, without being so tight as to 'bulge' out at the cheeks.
John L. Ashby.

Ch. Peachwoods Buttonfly Levi: Best of Breed at Westminster 1990 and 1991. Owned and bred by Virginia Gould, co-owner Kim Brinker, handled by Donald Rodgers. Here, the exhibit is being shown on the table. The lead is held behind the dog's ears, and the spare length is around the handler's neck, presenting a nice, tidy picture.

rarely defeated in breed classes. Sassy was a proper showgirl, oozing quality and that essential 'look at me' presence. She is also an example of how correct handling and presentation can enhance the overall picture. Obviously the more personality the dog has, the less this is required, but even those that 'show themselves' – or so the ringside believe – have to be cleverly 'handled'. Donald Rodgers, Sassy's handler on many occasions, is no stranger to top spots with his IG charges, including the blue and white Ch. Peachwoods Buttonfly Levi, co-owned by his breeder Virginia Gould and Kim Brinker. This dog was the Best of Breed Winner at Westminster in 1990 and 1991, he was Number One Italian Greyhound in 1990 and a multiple Group winner.

His parents are Ch. Pandee's Dandee and Pikop's Denim N Diamonds. Whelped on June 17th 1988 he is now the sire of Group winning and Group placing offspring himself. If you want to see greater numbers of Italian Greyhounds on show it is best to visit one of the Specialties, and the MidWest/Ravenna Specialty is a particular favourite for those in the breed. In 1991 there were 180 Italians entered in the Breed, Obedience and Parade of Champions. The following day at the Ravenna Kennel Club Show, the French judge Jean-Louis Grundheid had 131 IGs to assess. Best of Breed Westminster in 1992 was Ch. Silver Bluff Churchill Downs, handled by Miss Teresa Nail from Houston, Texas.

LEADING IG BREEDERS
The first time that an IG went Best in Show in the USA was in 1963 when Ch. Flaminia Of Alpine received the coveted award at the Santa Maria KC Show. The system of awarding titles means that there are numerically far more Champions in the USA and Canada than in the UK, and some kennels have been particularly dominant over the years. Ch. Dasa's King Of The Mountain (1978–1990) sired 78 Show Champions from 28 dams, and from the same kennel Ch. Dasa's Ebony Queen, born 1975, had a total of thirty Champion offspring by four different dogs. Both IGs were bred by Richard and Pat Sapp. In general, the litters in the USA are often larger than those in the UK in the present day. In the United States five in a litter is quite common, and often more, whereas in the UK the average size of litter is from one to four.

Registrations were first accepted in 1886 by the American Kennel Club, and the Italian Greyhound Club of America was formed in 1954. Numbers have fluctuated over the years in the same way as elsewhere, but the USA has sent many good Italian Greyhounds to the UK as well as importing from Germany, Italy, the UK and from the Austrian Springinsfeld kennel. The Aira Vana kennel, that was so useful to British breeders, was taken over by Mrs A. E. Dovelaar after the death of Mrs Norton, the original owner. It seems that Mrs Norton imported her foundation stock from England, from some of the best bloodlines, in approximately 1889. Aira Vana Phillipi was the first IG to win a Toy Group, in 1949.

In the same way that the UK benefited from stock from the USA, the reverse also applies. Three British imports each went on to sire a total of nine Champions. They were: Ch. Berinshill Dapper Dandy, born 8.4.1962 (Dante Of Velletri – Berinshill Paulina), Paolo Of Chelstoncross, born 9.3.1954 (Scipio Of Velletri – Can. Ch. Juliette Of Palermo) and Ch. Fleeting Feather In My Cap (Fleeting Noways Antonio – Fleeting Fritillary) born 8.23.1961. UK and Am. Ch. Ulisse Di Peltrengo, from Italy, had many Champion children. He is also behind the influential dog belonging to Ruth Bloore, Ch Wavecrest Veni Vidi Vici, a red and white male, born December 27th 1967, sired by Ch. Lyonhil's Roadrunner out of Wavecrest Demure Dimita. Ruth Bloore of the Wavecrest kennel bred her first Champion in 1952, and this was to be the first of many.

Ch. Wavecrest Veni Vedi Vici. Owned, bred and handled by Ruth Bloore. Sire of 42 Champions.

Ch. Tudor's Snow White and her son Ch. Tudor's Crystal Mountain, both solid white. Owned and bred by Susan Pinkus.

Lilian Barber (La Scala) and Ch. Venere Splende Di La Scala (unposed). Sired by Ch. Littleluv's Superman CD out of Olympia Di La Scala.

Bessie Scarlett, active in the breed in the UK in the 1900s, would have had a lot in common with Susan Pinkus, the owner of the 'Tudor' kennel in the USA, for Susan has achieved several generations of pure white Italians. Mrs Scarlett wrote that 'Lady in White', a 9lbs bitch, 13 inches high, born April 1890, was the only known white IG in the English Stud Book. Mrs Scarlett wanted to breed a white again and used the same line, as far as possible, and nearly succeeded. However, she wrote that "as War was breaking out and a change of address pending – all fell through." Susan Pinkus has evidently 'found' the right ingredients! In fact, her first white IG was a complete surprise, coming from a pied dam and a solid blue sire. This blue dog was descended from a brother of a white dog called Nanette's Snowberry, who was out of the von Bayerischen Meer line. Since then, they have just appeared. So far, Susan has not tried breeding two white parents together; the combination is usually white and coloured, but she certainly gets more than the average white progeny.

The first male that came to the Tudor kennels was Pretty Painted Elf, a pied son of the English dog, bred by Mrs M. B. Garrish, who became an American Champion called Fleeting Feather In My Cap. He was sired by Fleeting Noways Antonio out of Fleeting Fritillary. Antonio is a son of Ch. Noways Matthew, and Fritillary is a Matthew daughter out of Ch. Fleeting Chichele Atalanta. Born on August 23rd 1961, Elf's pedigree includes Ch. Dudolino Of Velletri, Noways Serenade Of Silvershowers, and the Canadian lines of the Palermos kennel.

A striking red and white dog called Ch. Tudor's Candy Man, currently in the kennel, not only

Ch. Littleluv's Sherlock Holmes (left) and Ch. Littleluv's Superman CD.
Owned and bred by Kathy Holmes.

has Feather In My Cap in his background but also another English import called Fleeting
Flambeau, who is his great grandsire. Flambeau was the litter mate to the CC winning Fleeting
Furore, who sired the black UK Ch. Fleeting Fine 'N Dandy. This is another example of the
wonderful colour range in the breed. One of the Tudor line was actually exhibited in the UK a
couple of times, but unfortunately the blue bitch Am. Ch. Tudor's Cinderella Navi Blu Of
Leander was not seriously campaigned. She was imported by Mrs Streatfield but transferred to
Mr P. Newman, well known for his Schnauzers, and she won a CC at the West of England
Ladies Kennel Society's Championship Show in 1978. There have, as I write, been over forty

Ch. Luisa's Set The Pace, owned by Mrs Louise Leschin. (Ch. Luisa's Cosimo of Bilair – Ch. Luisa's Call Me Viva Too). Foundation of this kennel was Imp. UK Am. Ch. Visconti Of Pequa and, from Italy, Ch. Sabina Del Calcione.

Ch. Colacove Diana The Huntress. Owned and bred by June Mastrocola.

Martin Booth.

Ch. KC's Ricardo Sebastiani: No. 1 IG in US 1989-1990 (Ch. Piacere's Guiseppe Victorio – Ch. Mira Sun Shadows). Winner of the Kal Kan award, 1990. Owned and bred by Charles and Kathleen Morgan, handled by granddaughter Kimberley Bakker.

home-bred Tudor IG Champions.

THE AMERICAN JUDGING SYSTEM
In the USA the exhibits have to enter one of the following classes, and it is interesting to note that the dogs already Champions do not have to meet others striving for their titles until the final competition. The classes are the same for each sex:
Puppy (can be broken down as 6-9 months and 9-12 months)
Novice
Bred By Exhibitor
American Bred
Open
   Each class has first, second, third and fourth places, assuming that there are sufficient entries. The first place winners are brought back into the ring, and the judge selects his winners. After selecting his winners, he then selects a Reserve Winner. He calls back the second place dog from the class that this winner came out of. This dog competes with the remaining first place winners for reserve. There are no points for reserve. The United States is divided into American Kennel Club geographical divisions, and each division has its own points systems.

CANADA

The Canadian Kennel Club set a similar set of conditions for a dog to attain the title of

Champion as in the USA, except that ten points under at least three different judges are required. The dog must either defeat another dog in its own breed or place in the Group with five or more breeds competing. Italians are in the Toy Group in Canada and the USA. The build-up to the Group is the same as the American process, except, of course, Canadian-bred classes as opposed to American-bred. In Canada the 'Canadian-Bred' classes are not carried beyond the Breed level, except as an option at Specialties. Points are won at the Winners level and are based on the number of dogs defeated; additional points can also be won at Group level, but only five points in total can be won at any one show.

Cece Haslam, who has researched the history of Italian Greyhounds in Canada, has found that although the breed has never been particularly popular, there has always been a nucleus of devoted fanciers, going back to the turn of the century when the recorded history of the Italian Greyhound in Canada began with the publication in 1889 of Volume I of the Canadian Kennel Club Registrations. The first two entries are:

522 Nellie, whelped Dec 28th 1888, fawn by Tip (imp) out of Nellie (imp). Owner H. Spackman, Exeter, breeder H. C. Burdick, Boston, Mass. (female).
523 Fritz Sultan, whelped April 7th 1889, fawn and white, by Drake (imp) out of Naughty (imp). Owner H. Spackman, Exeter; breeders Excello Kennels, Middleton, Ohio. (male).

In Volume II there is one IG recorded:

1894 Dainty Lass, female, fawn, born August 4, 1888, Miss Roberts, Pittsburgh, PA, USA. Owner R. P. Forshaw, Toronto, Ontario, sire Volna, dam Vixey. (Later Dainty Lass was recorded as owned by B. Davis and given a fresh number, 2799.)

After these first names appear the breed recurs in most Volumes in small numbers until 1953 when thirty were registered, twenty-nine of these carrying the Palermo prefix. This particular name is common among the pedigrees in other countries too. The early breeders included: Mrs T. W. Edwards, Toronto, Ontario (1906 to approximately 1916); Mrs S. A. Delaney, Toronto, Ontario (1913-1933) and the Palermo kennel-holder was F. D. Millar, London, Ontario (1939-1945). It seems that Mrs T. W. Edwards made an important purchase in 1909 from the UK. The British dog, Prince Ivanovitch, born June 12th 1906, sired by Prince Of Bampton out of Lady Of Fonthill, was to sire Victor T (registered in 1916), and he was the sire of twelve IGs between 1917 and 1924. Victor T, in turn, sired Lord Bobs (registered in 1920) who sired 27 IGs between the years 1921 and 1930. Lord Bobs was the sire of Blue Jacket (registered in 1928), and between 1929 and 1936 he is recorded as the sire of fourteen IGs. It seems from the Canadian records that Mrs Edwards was involved in breeding between 1906 and 1916, and the progeny continued to influence Italian Greyhounds some twenty years later. As the format for the information in the Canadian records was altered around 1915 to include only the name, registration number and sire, it is possible her involvement went further than that.

The British import Prince Ivanovitch had quite an adventurous life. Mrs Scarlett's diary, written in the UK, records that he was bought as a puppy from his breeder by Mrs Stafford Smith and then sold to a Mrs Mitchell in Dundee. Unfortunately it seems Mr Mitchell kept Dandie Dinmont terriers "who were likely to kill and eat him" – so he was advertised for sale. Mrs Scarlett reports: "Baroness Campbell saw the advertisement of this dog and wanted to see

Ch. Sheridanes Mikie (Sheridanes Glowing Rohan – Sheridanes Blue Velvet). Owned and bred by Ruth Bucknell.

Don Brown (left) with his English import Can. Ch. Turigner Gold Run and (right) Gold Run's daughter Broomhall's Golden Phoenix.

him on approval. I arranged the journey to London and paid expenses and cheque to be repaid later. The Baroness kept him about ten days, but before registering transfer said she did not wish to keep him, so I took him back. He came to London on February 19th, and to me on March 6th, 1908. A strong built dog, strong large head, too big for size of body, but of good greyhound shape and expression, very good correct small and tight ears. Long neck, well carried head, big in bone and rather coarse tail, inclined to carry gaily. Rather smutty bit on back. Big bone but not higher at the shoulder than Salto who looks much smaller and weighs lighter. (A good outcross for weedy, toyish under-bred bitches, who are too inbred and rickety.) Very quiet and affectionate but plenty of go."

He is described as a dark fawn, smut on back, black tail, two white toes off hind foot and a

IGs owned by D. and Anne-Marie Arthur (Scarra) pictured counter-clockwise from top left: Can. Am. Ch. Lelo's Paladin, Can. Am. Ch. Arabesque Anticipation, Can. Am. Ch. Scarra's Fascination, Can. Ch. Scarra Renaissance and Scarra's Excalibur.

little white on chest, and weighing about 10lbs. He sired a litter to Rosemead Vinca belonging to the Baroness, and the puppies apparently had long narrow heads, and were of very good greyhound type. In fact, two were sold for seven and eight guineas respectively – a fair price, I imagine, at the time. Prince Ivanovitch is then reported as being shipped to Mrs Edwards in Toronto on April 19th 1909 by Mrs Scarlett, who described him as: "Quite a good dog for stud and country shows, a bit coarse for London showing". The pedigree of Prince Ivanovitch is interesting, as his dam Lady Of Fonthill is noted as being Australian-bred.

Tilly van der Enz and Tilly who appear three generations behind her are from Germany, imported by Mrs Burger who bred IGs in the UK at this time. Midget I was born 1888 and was bred in New Zealand. Her owner Mrs Nicholson – the lady who bred Prince Ivanovitch – bought her in March 1890 in Australia; she was given away in 1896 and went to America! Aland, born in 1894, also belonged to Mrs Burger. These long sea journeys must have seemed interminable for these little dogs. Some of them seem to have travelled unaccompanied, and owners had to rely upon the good nature of the crew in charge to care for them.

An article in the American *Dog World,* written in the late 1970s by Vincent G. Perry, described how Mrs Delaney, who was well known for exhibiting her IGs in the Toronto area after the First World War and into the thirties, travelled to the shows on the street car with sometimes as many as a dozen dogs, all very well behaved and led on a multiple leash. Exhibitors used to rent box cars to travel between cities to the shows, and it must be concluded that the dogs' temperaments must have been very good to put up with it all. F. D. Millar registered two IGs in 1939: Anthony Of Palermo and Rogero Of Palermo.

In 1944 Pamelia Of Palermo was acquired by Charles F. Gilbert, who, in 1945, took on the transfer of the Palermo prefix. During the Second World War (1939-1945) all the Canadian registrations, with the exception of one American import, were Palermos. A total of 108 IGs were registered under this prefix between 1941 and 1961. The last that was registered was the bitch, Palermos Golden Salina. Ruth Bloore of the Wavecrest kennel in the US had a bitch and two dogs from this famous Canadian IG family: Gitano Of Palermos, Golden Flip and Pablo. Without doubt, they contributed to keeping the Italian Greyhound alive during these difficult times and were responsible for supplying the fresh stock needed in many other countries.

LEADING IG BREEDERS

The Canadian Italian Greyhound Association was formed in 1975 with twelve members and in 1977 the Association became a National Club, the Italian Greyhound Club of Canada, with a current membership of between twenty-five and thirty. Of the original members only three are still with the club: Marguerite O'Donnell (Eroseyrie) who was the first President, Cecelia Haslam (Sansegal), the Western Representative, and Ruth Bucknell (Sheridane), the Show Secretary. Boosters or Specialties have been held nearly every year since the club's inception. The three ladies above have been very loyal in their devotion to the breed and to the club. Mrs Bucknell, who began in dogs with Great Danes in 1949 and in IGs in 1972, founded her kennel with Ch. Paiga's Joy To The World, born in 1970 (Giovani's Soldatino D'Paiga – Paiga's The Painted One). Mated to Ch. Holiday's Mighty Mite, she produced Ch. Sheridane's Danti in 1983, who was not only a winner but a good sire of several Champions. Breeding has been limited, but seven generations later it is good to hear that Mrs Bucknell is commencing the puppy career of a youngster who goes back to one of her original line.

Marguerite O'Donnell and her late husband Donal started in the breed in 1960. Her foundation dog was Am. Can. Ch. Allegro Bravissimo Di Regio CD, born in 1969, who not only sired three Champions and was Number One IG in Canada in 1974, but was also the sire of Ch. Eroseyrie's Orio di Natale, born in 1978. The dam of this dog was an import from the UK, Can. Ch. Tamoretta Twilight. Her other English import, Ch. Tamoretta Teamspirit, litter sister to the well known British Ch. Tamoretta Tailormade, was Number Three IG in Canada in 1979.

Cecelia Haslam started in Miniature Poodles in 1960 and added IGs in 1972. She is no longer actively breeding or exhibiting, but no proof is needed of her loyalty to the breed or the club. Her first IG, called Ch. Copper Mist Samantha, born in 1971 (Copper Mist Sandalwood – Wavecrest Frivolity), was the dam of four Champions and two others pointed in Canada and the USA. The US import, Can. Ch. Luisa's Lady Blaise Piccicia, born in 1980 (Am. Ch. Luisa's Cosimo of

Ch. Luisa's Lady Blise Piccicia. Co-owners C. Haslam and L. Newbury; bred by Louise Leschin.

Ch. Newcourt Silver Touch with owner and breeder Mrs Louise Newbury of the Newcourt kennels.

Bilair – Am. Ch. Quarata Del Calcione) was co-owned with Louise Newbury, as was Can. Am. Ch. Sansegal's Alfa Romeo, a Group placer, both living with Mrs Haslam. The Newcourt prefix, belonging to Louise Newbury, Anne-Marie Arthur (Scarra), and Kathy Crane (Kabecca), have all owned and produced some lovely dogs on the Canadian scene.

Today the breed is in the capable hands of newer, but hopefully just as loyal breeders and exhibitors. One is Karen Chant (Diavolino) who started in IGs in 1985 with Ch. Pikop's Scandalous Affair, now the dam of two Champions and five more pointed. One of her latest is Ch. Diavolino's Lasting Impression, out of the same bitch and sired by Am. Can. Ch. Sunjata's Sunnyside Up, Number Two Top Winning IG in Canada 1989. Lasting Impression, a cream IG, is a multi Group placer and a Group Winner from the Senior Puppy Class.

Donald Brown started in the breed in 1985, and his import from the UK, Turigner Gold Run (now a Champion), bred by Barney and Rebecca Turner, actually came to visit me before his

Ch. Diavolino's Lasting Impression. Owned and bred by Karen Chant, co-owner Tracy Kerestesh.

flight back home with Don. It was a very 'international' day, as we had Jennifer Gielisse from Holland staying with us. It was a lovely English sunny day, with tea in the garden, and lots and lots of 'Italian' talk! Gold Run is sired by Ch. Tamoretta That's Talent out of Turigner Forget Me Not, and he now has progeny in the ring doing well too.

The future of the Italian Greyhound seems to be in safe hands in Canada. It is not bred in large numbers, and in the main IGs are kept in the homes of their owners and the majority are handled by their owners. The Breed Standard used in Canada was the same as the 1900 English version, but in 1987 revisions to part of it were made. More detail was given, and the rest is under revision as I write. The Canadian Breed Standard does include a ruling for height now, viz 13-15 inches (33-38cms), and any deviation from these limits must be considered a serious fault.

Chapter Nine

THE ITALIAN GREYHOUND WORLDWIDE

There have been different opinions regarding the classification of the Italian Greyhound from country to country. The earliest English language classification of dogs was made by Juliana Barnes, a Mother Superior, who in 1481 wrote the *Boke Of St Albans*. She did not apparently include Toy dogs. In Roman times six classes of canines were allocated i.e. Canes villatici (house dogs); Canes pastorales pecuarii (shepherd dogs); Canes venatici (sporting dogs]); Pugnaces or bellicosi (pugnacious or war dogs); Nares sagaces (dogs which ran by scent); Pedibus celeres (swift dogs which ran on sight). Various changes over the centuries have been made to these classifications and they have in turn varied from continent to continent. The Italian Greyhound appears in different Groups depending upon the arrangement of the classification by the governing Kennel Club of the country. Usually this is either the Toy Group (in the UK and the USA) or the Sighthound Group, but it may also be included in the Companion Group, or Non-Sporting Group. Opinions vary as to the most suitable Group for the Italian Greyhound. Because of its diminutive size some feel it should be in the Toy Group, others feel that as it is definitely a small hound, it should stand alongside its larger cousins.

ITALY

We all must be grateful to the many famous Italian artists for the beautiful paintings which depict Italian Greyhounds, a permanent reminder of the breed's popularity in Italy – the country which gave the breed its name, and believed by many to be the original home of the IG. Many important families of the aristocracy bred Italian Greyhounds for several generations, and in some instances the breed became more widespread because of marriages between noble families. Charles VIII of France, the son of Carlotta di Savria, had many IGs as pets and as hunting companions. The Holy Roman Emperor Maximilian, who married Mary of Burgundy, had his portrait painted with an Italian Greyhound. The Medici family were known to have owned many IGs. The breed's popularity in England was furthered through royal connections with Italy – Charles I of England was a son in law of Maria di Medici, and James II married an Italian Princess, Mary Beatrice of Modena. Other travellers during the 19th century, particularly gentlefolk on the 'Grand Tour', and some on business, brought back dogs from these old family

The late Marchesa Maria Luisa Incontri at home with her Italian Greyhounds.

Bali Del Calcione: one of the four IGs remaining at Calcione. F. Reed.

lines to their own countries. Baron Bartolazzi, whose daughters brought an Italian Greyhound called Adolphus to London in the late 1800s, had pictures of Italians in his villa in Italy, and it is believed that this strain had been kept for more than two centuries. The dogs were all pale in colour: pale fawn, cream, pale cream, pale golden, cream and white, and some were pure white. No black was suspected in the strain, and there were no black traces. All the dogs had dark brown or black nose. The inference of this is that there was no mixed blood in this strain at all. The baron's daughter, who was living in Rome in 1905, said that most of the old strains were extinct or very rare and it was difficult to obtain dogs of pure strain. There were still a few purebreds to be found in Milan, but the families were being weakened by inbreeding. Mrs Thring in the UK also writes that the Princess Helene D'Aosta reported in 1900 that pure Italian

Druso (Lotto 2 Del Calcione – Nuvola Del Calcione): Italian Ch., Club Ch., Stud Ch., European Ch., winner of fifteen CACs and twelve CACIBs. Owned by Agnese Spaziani.

Vertragus Erica (Ch. Vertragus Flavio – Freya Dei Piccoli Veltri) with her litter by Ever Blue De Shirkan, imp. France. Owned and bred by Aldo Cerletti, president of the Italian IG Club.

Ital. Ch. Frine Del Clan Della Zarina (Ch. Vertragus Lampo – Clarissa Del Clan Della Zarina) pictured at six years of age. Bred by Mirta Monari.

Greyhounds should not be confused with the small Greyhounds of Italy, commonly found in and around Naples and Sicily, which were usually grey, brown or black, with white feet and a star on the chest.

Luckily for us, the Marchesa Maria Luisa Incontri Lotteringhi della Stufa, renowned for her Del Calcione Italian Greyhounds in Italy, researched the subject well and her lovely book, although now out of print, is an excellent source of knowledge. My one regret is that I did not meet the lady personally, although I know several IG owners who talked to her over the years. Unfortunately the Marchesa died on January 1st 1991. She believed that the Italian Greyhound had been in existence in Italy since the time of the Etruscan and Roman civilisations, and her own 12th century palazzo, Il Calcione, once sketched by Leonardo Da Vinci, seems a very suitable backcloth for this old breed. The Marchese obtained her first Italian Greyhound in Bad Gastein, Austria, in February 1952 from the von Gastuna kennel. This was a bitch named Komtesse, and she was two years old.

Many lovely Italian Greyhounds followed, all were solid colours, as described in the FCI Breed Standard, which I believe she had a hand in compiling. She also helped form the Italian Greyhound Club in Italy. This was founded on November 21st 1956, and the Marchesa was President from 1958 until 1990. The aim of the club members was to breed good sound specimens, not frail and shivery, but able to appeal to all. In fact, it is thought in Tuscany in the fifties, some IGs were being used as hunting dogs. Evidently they were employed as beaters, and a field trial judge who saw them on a shoot said how surprising it was to see how well the Italians used their noses as well as their sight when working in cover. IGs are associated with the Sighthound group in many countries, but even in domestic circumstances you can see how an IG uses its nose to detect delectable morsels!

Sadly, with the death of the Marchesa, some of the remaining Del Calcione dogs were dispersed, but all went to caring owners including the current Secretary of the Italian Club, Agnese Spaziani. The granddaughter of the Marchese, breeds Sloughis in the main, but hopefully she will continue the line of her grandmother's lovely dogs. The Marchesa had a wonderful collection of statues of the breed, and she had a great knowledge and appreciation of art. Her love of all animals was indicated when on Saint Antonio's day in 1989 she invited all the people in the area to bring their animals to be blessed, with lunch in the castle after the blessing had taken place. All sorts of animals, including sheep, dogs, horses, pheasants, mynah birds, and a parrot attended the occasion. This talented breeder and judge was also a writer of excellent cookery books. She will be sorely missed not only by her husband, son and family, but by all involved with the Italian Greyhound.

Fortunately there are some Del Calcione Italian Greyhounds in other countries, and there are a number of owners in Italy who will hopefully continue to breed these lovely dogs in the country that gave them their name. Imports have been made from France in recent years, and only time will tell as to how the mixture will work. It is interesting to see that Gilberto Grandi, a keen Greyhound and Italian Greyhound owner, has a young Italian Greyhound, namely Sobers Emperia, bred by Astrid Jonsson and Bitte Ahrens out of their Swedish Ch. Sobers Tindra and sired by the South African and Swedish Ch. Cante Libre Quite Rightly of Bonne, who was in the UK for a while. This is another example of how widespread the breed has become, travelling overseas from the country which gave it its name, becoming successful in other countries, and then, ironically, returning to its first 'home' to inject new blood into the old lines. The breed is judged in acccordance with the FCI Standard.

THE NETHERLANDS
The Italian Greyhound was a favourite among the aristocracy in Holland during the eighteenth and nineteenth centuries, with travellers and diplomats playing a part in the movement and transportation of these small hounds. Their fortunes rose and fell, and in common with the breed elsewhere, were affected by the whim of fashion and the effects of World Wars. Just after the Second World War Mrs M. Donath-Seeuwen, who was a Dutch sighthound breeder and judge, added IGs to her kennel. Her kennel name of Bluedon's appears in almost every Italian Greyhound's pedigree in Holland, and many other European countries. IGs bred by Captain A. C. Stoel from Wassenaar and his Clocke v Damiate kennel and by Mrs P. H. Roodt at her Wismeyer's Aparts kennel also figure prominently. Imports were introduced from the Austrian, German and Swiss kennels to strengthen the gene pool, and thus the numbers and quality were assured.

Some of the early dogs were from Germany include: Lios Conny, male born April 28th 1950; Jenny von Silberfund, a brown and white bitch born October 19th 1951; Berry von St. Wendel, a fawn with white trim male, born June 23rd 1957 and Catja von St Wendel, a brown black female, with some white, born February 15th 1959, as well as Carin von St Wendel, her fawn litter sister. The first to arrive from the UK was Charsfield Gino, a light fawn male with white, born July 16th 1960, who was a son of Ch. Noways Matthew out of Noways Marla, bred by Mrs Peel. From America came Aira Vana's Figaro, an apricot fawn male, born May 1st 1962. The Springinsfeld kennel in Austria sent Nimrod and Nike, two blue grey male litter brothers, born August 21st 1963. Two more from America, born in 1964 and 1965 respectively were a bitch, Leewayne Bubble Of Jachelann, blue grey, and Black Lace Of Jachalann, a black and white dog. The first to arrive from France was Luigi Luciano Du Manoir Des Ombreuses, a fawn dog, born

ABOVE: First Il Piccolo Azzuro litter, Chico is pictured extreme right.

Chico Il Piccolo Azzuro: Ned., Int., Belg., Lux., Duits., Monaco Kamp 80, Eurokamp 82, Brabo w 78 en 82, CBRL w 80, Bundessg 79, Winner A'dam 79-80, NWC jaarprijs 79 en 82, World Champion 1979 and 1983, and his daughter Promessa Il Piccolo Azzuro.

Int. Dutch, World, Eng. Ch. Dairylane Moody Blue (Tamoretta Time After Time – Dairylane Pretty Flamingo) winning his title in Holland with Ms Jennifer Gielisse from judge R. Matheeuwson.

January 26th 1975. The Italian Greyhound in Holland is governed by the FCI Breed Standard, and, as there is no individual Breed Club, in 1975 it was decided that the breed should join the Whippet Club of the Netherlands with a representative on the board for Italians. I have been fortunate to meet many of the Dutch exhibitors both in Holland and on their visits to the UK. One of the most successful IG breeders is Ms Jennifer Gielisse and her 'Il Piccolo Azzuro' kennel. She started in Italians in 1975, and her first litter in April 1977 produced six puppies including Chico Il Piccolo Azzuro, who achieved eighty-four Championships in ten different countries under forty-five different judges, including the World title in 1979 and 1983.

His sons Othello (black) and Stefano (grey) have followed on in similar pattern, both winning and siring many other good Italians. It was to this home that my own Ch. Dairylane Moody Blue travelled after winning his title in the UK. He won the World title for his new mistress in 1991 bringing the Il Piccolo Azzuro kennel's total at this premier show to seven World Champion titles with five different Italians, Best of Breed seven times, plus the World Junior title eight different times with eight different Italians. There is a predominance of black and blue in this kennel, and Chico's grandfather was the French import Luigi Luciano.

The solid colouring required by the FCI Breed Standard is obviously observed in Holland, and there are a number of breeders who breed mainly fawns. Imports have come from various other countries, more recently, Poland and France, and the Dutch breeders have also been responsible for many good exports. On my visits to Holland I have been impressed by the fact that the exhibitors there keep their dogs in the ring much longer than in the UK. For some reason the British dogs seem to disappear at three to four years of age, and often do not appear again until the Veteran classes (seven years) or in the non-competitive Champions Parades at Club events.

I also admire the breeders classes and team classes that seem to be such a feature of the Championship shows in Holland and other European countries, providing quite a spectacle, where handlers may have several of their chosen breed on display together. Teams of Italians shown in this way competing with the other breeds certainly catch the eye and give a very good insight into the overall depth of quality of a kennel, both with regard to looks and temperament. Many owners participate in lure coursing and racing with their Italian Greyhounds and enjoyable days are spent with the other sighthound owners.

BELGIUM

Mevr Leona Dams Reynaert says that as a breeder and judge she thinks the most important aspect of an Italian Greyhound is its overall, general appearance and its gait. Obviously governed by the FCI Standard she stresses that in her opinion the movement should *not* be high-stepping nor straight like a Whippet. There must be elegance in the movement, and it should be springy and elastic.

I had the pleasure of judging some of this lady's dogs some years ago in Holland, and I made her Helios Of Devils Pigeons Best of Breed and Best Dog, and he was later Best in Show. His sire was Ch. Petit Prince de la Perle Grise – Olympe des Pitchoun Diables. He was a lovely golden fawn male. Racing and coursing is followed by IG owners in Belgium and I know that Francoise and Philippe Duponcheel-Vandenbussche course with their little 'Gregorio' and get great enjoyment out of this. These IG owners have also found a wealth of information concerning the paintings where the breed is featured, and a number of articles on the subject have been written for the Breed Club in Belgium.

Ned., Lux., Int., Europ., Ch. Hera of Devils Pigeons with Madame Dams-Reynaert.

GERMANY

There is no individual Breed Club for Italian Greyhounds in Germany, although there is a club for all breeds of sighthounds called the D.W.Z.R.V. (Deutscher Windhund Zucht und Rennverband) with a representative for Italians, who for some time has been Waltraud Peschger, who is a Championship Show judge for all sighthound breeds. IGs in Germany are included in the Sighthound Group for classification purposes. The Stud Book of Registrations for the breed began in 1910 with 120 included. The first IG to be registered was a bitch called Alma Von Obermenzing born June 29th 1908; the second is also a bitch, born January 1st 1898. Currently they are up to number 2933. The breed is governed by the FCI Standard and the dogs take part in conformation and racing competition.

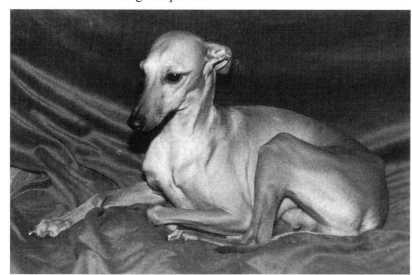

Figaro De Shirkan: this IG competes on the race track and in the show ring in France. Owned by Evelyne Diacquenod.

FRANCE

The Club Francais du Petit Levrier Italien was formed in 1960 by Madame Simeon-Lavallard, with Madame Tuma as President. Italians compete in both beauty and racing competitions, and enthusiasts hope that their dogs will gain titles in both fields. Madame Evelyne Diacquenod and her De Shirkan kennel has French, Swedish and Austrian lines in the pedigrees.

SCANDINAVIA

In Scandinavia the Italian Greyhound is placed in the Sighthound Group and a good place to see them on exhibition is at the big Championship Sighthound Show in the summer at Skokloster. The Scandinavian countries are governed by the FCI Standard and therefore the restrictions within it govern their choice of colour. Astrid Jonsson of the Sobers Kennel has been a keen exhibitor and breeder of the Italian Greyhounds for a great many years, and she imported the first black Italian to be seen in Sweden in 1963 from Mr and Mrs Morgan of the UK. She was called Nagrom Magica (Nagrom Merlo – Ch. Nagrom Carima) and turned out to be a fabulous

Pictured left to right: Ch. Sobers Falene, Sobers Zanzara, Int. Nord. Ch. Sobers Patena and Sobers Curiosa.   *E. Rasehorn.*

brood bitch, becoming the dam of six Champions including one American Champion. As well as producing their own lines, two Berinshill bitches from the UK have been very influential in Scandanavia: Nordic Ch. Berinshill Timoshenka and Int. Nord. Ch. Berinshill Amaranda (a daughter of Ch. Nadilee Red Chiffon of Berinshill). Recently the Uk import Atina Christian gained his title.

In Norway S. N. Ch. Fleeting Flora-Dora, bred by Mrs M. Garrish, has produced many winning offspring at the May Day Sols kennel including Nord. Ch. Seawards Sapphire Blue (Eng. Ch. Fleeting Firefly – Totem Folly) who was the top winning IG in Norway in 1987. Ch. Sobers Patena was a lovely bitch and a great favourite with all round judge Lionel Hamilton-Renwick from the UK and many other International judges. Imports have come in from Australia from Ken Smith of the Minaken kennel. Some of the puppies may initially bring in a different type to that usually seen, but it is hoped that the good things from both sides will produce some top quality Italians. The pedigrees contain many international kennel names e.g. Philtre and Tentyra (UK); Wavecrest (USA); Minaken (Australia); Calcione (Italy), plus the Swedish Sobers lines. The granddaughter of Mrs Jonsson, Ms Bitte Arhrens, is now the regular handler for the Sobers kennel and she tells me that their dogs love lure coursing at the Saluki Club's venue in Stockholm.

Italian Greyhounds are far from being a common sight in Denmark; at the present time only three breeders are registered. Kirsten Kristensen and her 'Vindhause' kennel have probably done more than most over the past two decades at keeping the breed alive and the quality high.

Pictured left to right: Int. Ch. Dk. Ch. P1Ch. K1BCh. Il Cagnolino Alvaro ; Int. Ch. Dk. Ch. P1Ch, K1B Ch. Il Cagnolino Angelica, Int. Ch. Dk. Ch. VDH Ch. Bianca, Dk. Ch. K1B Ch. Il Cagnolino Belizza and Vindhauses Giovanna.   *B. Bjorch.*

Kirsten is to be congratulated on her persistent desire to breed quality IGs. During the eighties Ruth Broustbo 'Ronnaes' also bred IGs with foundation dogs from Kirsten, but unfortunately it seems she is not currently active in breeding Italians. Few litters are born and three to seven puppies have been the average registered over the last five years (as at 1993).

The Sobers kennel in Sweden has been an important influence in Denmark, and Int. Ch. Nordic DKCH Sobers Gossair, a son of Ch. Sobers Patina, the top winning IG in Sweden, now lives with the other Vindhause dogs. Some out-crosses have been made with dogs from Holland and Germany. One of the more recent owners is Susie Bjorch, in partnership with her mother, who registered the kennel name 'Il Cagnolino' in 1987. As her parents owned a Doberman Pinscher and an Irish Wolfhound the contrast is quite dramatic! Their first IG was Int. DKCH VDHCH Bianca, bred by Ruth Broustbo and with Vindhause parents. Douglas Appelton awarded this bitch the first Certificate towards her Danish title at only her third show. She was top IG in Denmark twice, and runner-up twice. A second IG puppy followed in 1986 from Kirsten Kristensen. This bitch, named DKCH Vindhauses Giovanna, also got her title.

The next step was to breed a litter. Bianca was mated to Gossair, and as he was still in Sweden at the time, semen was imported. One puppy resulted, to be known as DKCH KLBCH Il Cagnolino Belizza, and in the autumn of 1991 she went Group 1 and Best in Show 2 at a large show, which is the best result ever for an Italian Greyhound in Denmark. Currently six Italians share the Bjorch home, and it is good to hear of the encouragement and support given by both the top kennels, Vindhause and Sobers, to these new enthusiasts. Hopefully more support for the breed will be given, as Mats Pedersen moved house in 1990 from Sweden to Denmark with his Elkjhor Whippets and Italian Greyhounds.

Italian Greyhounds are not used for racing or coursing at all in Denmark, and until Il Cagnolino Angelica and Alvaro arrived on the scene, there were none in obedience competition. These IGs were the first to win Class 1 in Denmark and later Alvaro also won a Class 2. Angelica and Alvaro are the first to venture into this type of competition, which follows the same basic format as elsewhere, so it will be interesting to see if others follow. Ms Bjorch is definitely of the opinion that IGs have more brains than sometimes they are credited with, but these clever and intelligent little dogs do require a lot of understanding to work them in obedience. However, the satisfaction of the close rapport achieved makes all the effort well worthwhile.

Finland has a small but devoted band of IG owners. As well as breeding their dogs for the beauty and conformation ring, there is also a growing interest in using them for lure coursing. Many sighthounds course in Finland, but although Italian Greyhounds are included in the sighthound group they run separately, but under the same set of rules. There are lure coursing titles to be won, and several IGs are well on the way to gaining these honours. Minaken Marksman (bred by Ken Smith in Australia) and Taikatyon Tuulispaa are, to date, the only double Champions holding their breed title and lure coursing titles, but it seems more are set to follow with excellent speeds. I understand they are not as fast as the English Greyhounds, but some have proved they can be faster than Irish Wolfhounds and in some instances almost as fast as the Afghans who usually record good speeds over the 280 metre stretch, with speeds of approximately 22 seconds.

AUSTRALIA

How Italian Greyhounds arrived in Australia is one of the mysteries that surround the breed. Could it be some of the rather more wealthy early settlers took their dogs with them? Or perhaps some of the Merchant vessels exploring this continent exchanged them in return for goods? Italian Greyhounds were certainly highly prized in the early nineteenth century, and would, no doubt, have commanded a high exchange rate.

These long sea voyages with the accompanying hazards of storms and other calamities took their toll on the human travellers, and therefore it is inevitable that some of these little dogs would have perished. Yet, there is no doubt that many dogs travelled in order to accompany their owners, and a number reached Australian shores. Early show records indicate that Italian

Greyhounds were at the Sydney Royal Show between 1868 and 1900, with the females officially recorded as 'sluts'! The fashion for the smaller IG was obviously the vogue in Australia too, as in 1873 'Beauty', who was a year old, was 12 inches in height and only weighed 6lbs. The last entry recorded in New South Wales for that period was Topsy, in 1899, who was seven years old. I think her owners must have had a sense of humour, as it is written that her sire was Sting and her dam Nettle!

IGs were also being exhibited in South Australia and Victoria in the 1880s, and it is generally assumed that they were in Tasmania and maybe Queensland at this time. Records indicate the Italian Greyhound seems to have disappeared from the show catalogues after 1900. This was possibly due to the same reason as for their decline in the UK, with the unappealing characteristics resulting from the desire for ever-smaller dogs.

However, it is established that in 1958 Mrs Sapio of the Cruchfield Kennels in Queensland, imported Chichele Proserpina and Noways Hermes from the UK. Their first litter were named after the Three Graces – Eufrosine, Aglaia and Talia. Talia was to join the home of Barbara Skilton of the El Tazzi prefix, in Tasmania, and Aglaia was the foundation of the kennel in Victoria known as the Althahallach Italians. Apparently Mrs Sapio exhibited her dogs in Brisbane in the late fifties, and the first home bred El Tazzi IG, named El Tazzi Anna Maria, appeared at the Sydney Royal in 1962.

Mrs Sapio imported several other Italians from the UK in an effort to establish the breed in Australia. These included Noways Mark (Ulisse Di Peltrengo of Winterlea – Noways Editie Clocke Damiate) bred in the UK by Mrs M. Barnard, and litter brother to Eng. Ch. Noways Matthew. When mated to Chichelle Proserpine (Noways Starlight – Ch. Golden Arrow Of Velletri) – also from the UK and spelt as Prosperina in some records – bred by Mrs Rieley, they produced her Ch. Cruchfield Nefertiti. This bitch was the first top winning IG in Australia, and her many good wins included runner-up to Best in Show at Brisbane Royal in 1964.

It is interesting to look at the pedigree of this bitch. Ulisse Di Peltrengo Of Winterlea was imported by Mrs M. Mooney (UK) from the Marchese Montecuccoli in Italy (Simba Springinsfeld from Frau Pia Pfleger in Austria – Ombretta di Peltrengo). Noways Editie Clocke Damiate was a bitch imported from Holland by Mrs Barnard from her breeder Capt. A. C. Stoel. Damiate's sire was Falk.V. Schloss Richmond, and her dam was Jenny V. Silberfund Winster. The sire of Ch. Golden Arrow Of Velletri had been imported from Germany from Frau Baronin von Woyrsch in 1949 to the UK by Mrs Massey Cooke and her daughter Mrs C. Howard, and his name was Agnesina Savelli. Quite a combination as you can see!

Two other IGs of note who joined Mrs Sapio's kennels in the 1960s were Berinshill Russet Rose, bred by Diana Waugh, and the Challenge Certificate winning Philtre Gino, bred by Rae Lewis, both from the UK. Gino became a Champion in his new country and sired some nine Champions. He had already been proven at stud in the UK before his journey, siring the lovely Ch. Philtre Florena.

Noways Dinkie (Noways Starlight – Canadian Ch. Noways Palermos Twinkling Star) born in 1955, was bred in the UK by Mrs Barnard and transferred to Miss D. M. Boyd and apparently accompanied her mistress to New South Wales. Dinkie was mated to Noways Mark and produced a dog called Pickett Willem Ruys and a bitch called Pickett Merrylegs. Both went to Mrs Sapio when Dinkie returned to the UK with her owner. Willem later joined the El Tazzi kennel, and in 1961 he was shown at Melbourne Royal for a Challenge and BoB. After Talia was taken to Tasmania a few IGs were shown during the 1960s and early 1970s, often winning at

Ch. Rathburn Ragtime Gal, owned by Mrs Blackburn. (Ch. Tudor's White Gold imp. USA – Ch. Corcloon Mindy). Tudor's White Gold was sired by Fleeting Flambeau of Cleden, imported from the UK.

Ken Smith and Ch. Minaken Special Blend (Ch. Hyjinx Supa Dupa imp. UK – Ch. Minaken Rambling Rose).

Group level. When the El Tazzi kennel moved to New South Wales very little breeding was undertaken, and it was several years before IGs were shown again, and then only in ones and twos, and this applies even now.

Victoria was the place that the breed became most firmly established with entries steadily climbing to sixty-one at the 1974 Royal Show. Since then they seem to have maintained an average of thirty to forty entries. David Roche, from South Australia, was in England to jointly judge Best in Show at Crufts with Mr Gilliat, and he visited Mrs P. Heap to purchase a puppy bitch. At the same time he agreed to take Chandrey Gianna, born in 1968 (Ch. Estrada Blondin – Chandrey Lavinca) who was for sale, and he eventually persuaded Mrs Heap to allow Chandrey Palestra to go too. This bitch had recently won her Junior Warrant, one of the first IGs to do so.

Ch. Shaaltarah Last Waltz
(Ch. Shaaltarah Cesare –
Ch. Shaaltarah Lucretia).
Owned by Mrs Mary Keast,
bred by Mrs L. Schelling.

Ch. El Tazzi Lucky Strike
(Ch. Batik Merceller – Ch.
Ellaway Salomi Sprite),
owned and bred by
Mr F. and Mrs B. M.
Skilton.

Mr Roche also imported Medlif Bella Maria, as well as the two Chandrey bitches from England. Maria was bred by Mrs Grant (Philtre Fabrizo – Medlif Tinkerbell), born in 1968. Maria's children became fairly widespread throughout Australia, but offspring from the Chandrey bitches remained in Victoria and South Australia. In South Australia the breed is not shown consistently; the majority are kept purely as pets and very little breeding takes place.

In Western Australia the first IG recorded was El Tazzi Antonio (Noways Mark – Talia) in 1961. Later the Ardmore Kennels obtained dogs from the Bela kennels in Queensland, which was founded on Cruchfield stock from the early imports. In Queensland the breed has fluctuated in numbers over the years, but nowadays there are a few breeders who are more consistent and show and breed litters on a more regular basis. There have been Italians in the Northern Territory from time to time since the 1960s, but Wondoan Jazz was the first to be shown to his title in 1981.

In New South Wales there were a few keen owners who kept the flag flying with Italians, and in April 1980 the Italian Greyhound Society was formed with Mrs B. Skilton of the El Tazzi prefix as President and David Sales as Hon. Secretary. The Society has formed very close links with the other Breed Clubs in the UK and USA. This Society is still the only specialist club for the breed in Australia and the membership embraces all States and New Zealand. The Annual Championship Show has entries from most States. There was a record entry for the breed in Australia at the 1989 Speciality Show when Lillian Barber (La Scala) from the USA judged.

One of the more recent imports to the El Tazzi kennel was Ch. Turigner Creme Soda, bred by Mrs and Miss Turner in the UK. He was born in 1979 and died in October 1991. He was sired by Ch. Tamoretta Tidalwave Of Turigner, who was a son of Ch. Tamoretta Tailormade. He was not extensively used at stud in Australia but produced fourteen Champions, and several other good winning children. This made him the top Champion producing IG stud dog ever in Australia. Berinshill Mark Anthony was exported from the UK and Berinshill Merry Monarch is one of the later UK imports who has proved an asset, but it is too early to assess his input on the breed.

Currently the Italian Greyhound is exhibited under the UK Breed Standard, accepted by the Australian National Kennel Club. However, this governing body has recently decided to become affiliated with the FCI. This means a conflict in the requirements of the Breed Standard, as compared with the British Breed Standard with regard to colours and movement. There are many lovely specimens of Italian Greyhounds in Australia, already holding the title of Champion, who are in a delightful range of colours and whose action is decidedly high-stepping, so the effect on the breed could be dramatic.

I understand that at present the ANKC have advised the Italian Greyhound Society in Australia that although affiliated to the FCI, they have not as yet adopted the FCI Breed Standard, and if this happens they have indicated that a compromise would be reached where Standards differ to a major degree. It would be a pity if this change in the ANKC's direction influenced the breeding of Italian Greyhounds, as breeders have been able to take advantage of stock from the USA and the UK and have thus enlarged their gene pool. It would seem heartless to disregard the efforts of the many dedicated breeders, and I cannot think the authority would allow this to take place. Only time will tell.

Using the method of Southern Australia as an example, the dogs are judged on a points system. Five points for a Challenge Certificate (or CC) and one for the exhibit. A total of one hundred points are needed for a Champion title, and a maximum of twenty-five can be won at any one show. If the dog wins a Group, twenty-five points are awarded instead of those already achieved from its breed wins. In popular breeds, such as the Cavalier King Charles Spaniel, if there were one hundred entries, twenty-five points are still the maximum. But it means, in theory, a dog could gain its title at four shows from its classes. In the less popular breeds it takes a lot longer – a rare breed such as an Affenpinscher may need seventeen CCs to get its one hundred points because of the small entries. Obedience titles have also been won by several IGs.

SOUTH AFRICA

When Nicola Of Velletri and her litter brother Valentino Of Velletri were bred by Mrs Massey Cooke in the UK on February 19th 1960 no one could have known that they would be making the long journey to South Africa. Purchased by Michael Hughes-Hall and Bill Campbell-Martin respectively, they were the first imports to the country some thirty years ago. These two pups were sired by Primo – Grisell Of Velletri, and Primo went back to Brucemiks Sam who had come from the USA to the UK. Later they made two imports from Mr and Mrs D. Morgan in the UK: Nagrom Scherzo (Nagrom Bruno – Nagrom Di San Siro, born April 2lst l961) and Nagrom Francesco, another Bruno daughter out of Nagrom Bertuccia, born on February 12th 1962. The litter was very much based on the Italian imports that the Nagrom kennel had introduced to the UK. Messrs Hall and Campbell-Martin also had two bitches, bred by Mrs Galloway in 1961, called Carla Maria and Irma la Duce. They were based on Honeygaze and Chichele lines in the UK, which again had foreign blood behind them.

A Mrs Taylor bought Estrada Aramis from Messrs J. H. Scholes and R. Street in England, and later there were imports from the English kennels of Berinshill and Philtre – Berinshill Wild Chance and Philtre Felini. Mrs Martin contacted breeders in the USA and Falotica's La Giaconda joined the kennel. It has to be said that some of these imports were fairly closely related and therefore the gene pool was still quite small, which is always a problem in the relatively uncommon breeds. Ms Sylvia de Klerk has imported a Dasas bitch from the USA, which is one of the top kennels and Alison Parkhouse has imported several good dogs from the UK and the USA over the last seventeen years.

Two IGs, Narrabo Jumping Jouster and Eng. Ch. Narrabo Sweet 'N Neat, have come from the Narrabo kennel belonging to Dr and Mrs D. Smith in the UK. It is interesting to note that this was in the early 1980s, and in 1989 a son of Jouster, who is now a South African Champion, returned to the UK. He is called Canta Libre Quite Rightly Of Bonne, and after siring some winning stock in the UK and gaining a CC, he went on to the Sobers kennel in Sweden where he quickly gained his Swedish title. Quite Rightly had an American-bred dam from the Dasas kennel. Mrs Parkhouse has also imported from the Runners, Laviere and Dei Carini kennels in the USA, and although at first sight these imports may appear far reaching, in fact they all go back to her Karam and di Regio lines. Peggy Miller in South Africa has a large houseful of Italian Greyhounds, and has always been a keen supporter of the breed. Mrs P. Spencer, who returned to the UK in the 1980s, brought her Italians with her, including S. Af. Ch. Rilloby Figleaf Of Cante Libre, and has been very successful breeding her to English bloodlines.

The Italian Greyhound in South Africa is judged in accordance with the UK Breed Standard, which varies little from that of the USA, and can therefore make use of all the varying colours of Italians enjoyed by the prefixes already mentioned. To become a Champion in South Africa a dog needs to win five Challenge Certificates under five different judges, with one Certificate won at any away centre (this means at a show held in a province other than where the exhibitor lives), and also one Challenge Certificate has to be won after the exhibit is over eighteen months of age. Reserve Challenge Certificates are awarded, but they do not contribute in any way to a dog being called a Champion.

Champions are usually shown in the Champions' class, although it is not against the rules to show in the Open class. Few do this, however, and therefore other dogs who have not yet been awarded their Championship title rarely have to meet reigning Champions, making the path towards gaining a CC a little smoother. Occasionally an exhibitor will make a stand and exhibit their dog in the Open class, although it already has its title, in an effort to make the competition keener, but this is apparently quite rare. The Champion and those being campaigned for their title only meet after the classes when there is a challenge for Best of Breed.

Any serious breeder or exhibitor in the Cape Province has to be ready, willing and able to travel extensively to campaign their dogs as there are only seven Championship Shows held

Ch. Laviere Daisies Don't Tell at Canta Libre (Ch. Dasa's Eye of the Tiger – Ch. Laviere Midnight Fantasy). Bred by Jamie Daly, USA. Top Toy Dog South Africa 1988, Top Bitch South Africa All Breeds, No. 11 All Breeds. Won over twenty Groups.

Ch. Canta Libre Just an Inkling (Ch. Dasa's Born In The USA – Canta Libre Stirling Star), bred by Alison Parkhouse. Multi Group winner at Championship Show level.

there. The majority of the dog shows takes place in the Transvaal and there are Open or Championship Shows most weekends from March to October. Dog shows are also held in Durban, Port Elizabeth, East London, Grahamstown, Kimberley and Bloemfontein. Johannesburg is 1000 miles from Cape Town, for instance, and it takes about fourteen hours driving or two hours flying. Exhibitors certainly have to be dedicated to undertake such travel with their little dogs. No Championship shows are held from mid November to the end of February because it is considered too hot for the dogs.

There are a number of Special Events held that sound a great deal of fun and have a number of different fancy titles. Registrations of IGs are in the order of about twenty-five dogs a year, and compared with other toy breeds this is not many. For example, from September 1990 to August 1991 there were twelve IGs registered, 430 Chihuahuas, 452 Maltese, 1148 Yorkshire Terriers, 447 Pomeranians, and 420 Pekes. Nevertheless, despite this handicap the Italian Greyhounds usually manage to be amongst the breeds winning at the highest level.

Chapter Ten

OBEDIENCE TRAINING

Most Italian Greyhound enthusiasts are attracted to the breed for its beauty, its elegance and its engaging personality. Few are aware of its intelligence and even fewer attempt to train it to competition level of Obedience.

Sandra Birch, Sue Dunning and Penny Rose are among the few IG owners who have attempted training in the UK, apart from Pam Heap (Chandrey) who went to Canada in 1979 and stayed for ten years and has brought back two CD trained Italians. Her Can. Ch. Glenairley Chandrey Adamo, CD (Adam) is a black dog with white trim, and he won his CD (Companion Dog) at the Greater Victoria Dog Obedience Training Club Trials in June 1989 under judge Ivy Campbell. He was bred by Mrs J. W. Anderson and is sired by Am. Ch. Gogi's Bronze Buckwheat and is out of Glenairley Chandrey Laura. Laura has two Canadian Champions as her sire and dam, namely Can. Ch. Chandrey Cortigiano and Can. Ch. Wavecrest Misty. I have had a very brief demonstration of him doing basic Obedience and was most impressed. He still attends Obedience classes with his owner for recreation, now they are back in the UK, and I know Mrs Heap enjoys this with him far more than the beauty side of competition. Mrs Heap is hoping to continue his progress in competition and they are an important part of the display team of the training club they belong to in Yorkshire.

Glenairley Chandrey Lark (born April 29th 1981), owned by Mrs Heap when she was in Canada, was also bred by Mrs Anderson. This IG absolutely hated the conformation classes. She was therefore introduced to Obedience, and won her CD in 1984. Sadly, little Lark only had a couple of years in the UK, originally in quarantine, and then back with her mistress before she died. She will be sadly missed by her owner and by Adam, but her ashes will be buried beneath a Victoria plum tree that is in their garden, befitting a little IG that was born in Victoria, Canada.

Sandra Birch feels it is important to ask around about local training clubs and visit before you take your IG, as some trainers will not have met one before and you may feel they are not best-suited to the breed. It is best to take the IG for a visit initially, so it can get the feel of the hall. Never let the trainers push you and your Italian on at a faster rate than you feel the dog can cope with. All breeds are so different from each other. The dog must definitely enjoy it and the outing should be pleasurable for dog and owner. All dogs can get bored with training, but Italians do so

Pictured left to right: Can. Ch. Glenairley Chandrey Adamo CD, his dam, Glenairley Chandrey Laura and Glenairley Chandrey Lark, recently deceased.

very easily. One suggestion is that for retrieve a soft leather glove stitched into a square is a suitable article to practise with, and to be used after every exercise as a game. Sandra Birch and her Narrabo Silent Knight were very enthusiastic as a team and he performed very well in competition.

Sue Dunning has done basic Obedience training with all of her IGs, but Philtre Federigo is the one who has proved the most successful. The South Eastern Toydog Society is the only society in the UK which specifically provides classes for Toy dogs in Obedience as well as scheduling breed classes. Philtre Federigo actually won the Pre-beginners class at one of their Limited shows. His 'Down' stays are a source of great amusement as he prefers to be on his back with all his legs in the air. Apparently he has been described as a set of bagpipes that has been thrown to the ground! The exercises are all the same as for the larger breeds.

Sue has found retrieving a problem with Federigo, for while he will accept the dumb-bell from her if she runs too, when it is thrown for him to fetch, the look he gives her says it all: "You threw it – you fetch it!" She has taken the plunge and entered him in 'proper' competition with this exercise, but after watching intently where she threw the dumb-bell, he ran straight out of the ring, across the field and into the next field to a distant telegraph pole – where he promptly relieved himself and then looked for his owner. Feeling rather foolish, Sue continued with the exercise as if all was normal, and she dutifully 'called' her dog and he did the longest, straightest, fastest recall she has ever seen! The fun sport of Agility is fast catching on everywhere, and Helen Davis has experimented with this type of training with her IGs – another example of the capabilities of the Italian Greyhound.

In North America the Italian Greyhound fraternity have developed the art of Obedience training, and with patience, hard work and determination, some dogs have achieved surprising

Sue Dunning preparing Philtre Federigo for the recall.

Danny at attention – Ch. Uwharrie's Wild About Red CDX, owned by Nicole Howland.

levels of success. Karen Langenbrunner from Ohio, contributes the following insight into this aspect of Italian Greyhounds:

"The concept of Obedience has been around since before the time of Christ: 'The reason I wrote you was to see if you would stand the test and be obedient in everything' 2 Corinthians 2:9 (NIV). From children obeying their parents to animals obeying their masters, 'training' is the means to achieve this goal. Dog Obedience is a popular and fast-growing fancy in the United States and Canada. However, the Italian Greyhound in Obedience remains a rare treat to watch. While not having the pure drive of a Border Collie, or the animation of a Golden Retriever in the ring, they possess all these qualities in their own way, plus an elegance and grace that none of the 'popular' breeds can match. Obedience is a hobby the entire family can enjoy and participate in. A handler can be nine or ninety, it doesn't matter. The common bond is that they care for their dog and they enjoy the sport.

"The IG owner certainly can't chase and catch his dog, so the dog must be trained to come to him on command. Most enthusiasts start taking 'Fido' to a basic Obedience class, usually offered by a local training club, because the dog won't come when he's called or he drags his owner down the street when he's walked on a leash. After eight to twelve weeks of daily practising with a step-by-step schedule, the owner is pleased with how Fido is transformed before his very eyes.

"The bond between owner and dog has deepened and the owner starts wondering how much more can Fido do? He sees advanced dogs walking miraculously by their owner without a leash, jumping hurdles, and fetching things on command. Could Fido do this? They join the local training club, and very soon daily training sessions and a weekly training night 'out with the dogs' are commonplace. The words 'fun matches', 'titles', and 'legs' start creeping into the vocabulary and before you know it, Fido and his owner are fully-fledged Obedience enthusiasts.

"Any dog can compete in Obedience. The IG can be a Champion blue blood or rescued from the local Animal Shelter. Mixed breeds may not be able to compete in licensed Obedience trials, but they can compete in fun matches. In the USA, licensed trials can be sanctioned by the American Kennel Club or the United Kennel Club. More recently, the States Kennel Club is coming into popularity. The Canadian Kennel Club is the main registry for Canada. A pure-bred dog must be registered with the specific Kennel Club that you want to show in and obtain titles from. There are three different training levels dogs can progress through in all of the Kennel Clubs: Novice (primary school level), Open (secondary school), and Utility (university level). Slight variations exist among the Kennel Clubs as to the specific exercise, but the overall basics remain the same.

"A team of handler and dog walks into the ring with a perfect score of 200 points. Just as in the Olympics, as the team is put through their routines by a judge, points are deducted for each error made. To obtain a 'leg' or qualifying score towards a title, a minimum score of 170 points must be earned, including at least half the points in each of the exercises performed. Generally, qualifying scores (legs) must be earned in three different trials, judged by three different judges, to earn the Obedience title at each level. Some Kennel Clubs require only two different judges, but still at three different trials. There is no time limit.

"Before any exercise is taught, Fido must first learn 'attention' – that is, looking directly at the handler and focusing all of his attention on his human. Dogs must 'think' about what they are doing in the ring. If they are distracted and their concentration is broken, the results could range from a few points off to non-qualifying. They must be able to return their attention back to the handler to regain their composure and thought process quickly. Let us use the American Kennel Club scoring system as an example.

"In all Kennel Clubs, the exercises vary in difficulty with each level. In Novice routines, each team must heel a pattern on leash including a fast pace, slow pace, right and left turns, and reverses of directions with several halts thrown in. A figure eight is then done around two human posts. So far, the exercises have been worth 40 points. A common fault with the Italian Greyhound in heeling is 'weaving'. It's hard to channel all of that energy into a direct parallel line with the handler's pace!

"Next the leash comes off and the dog must stand still with the handler approximately six feet away, while the judge touches Fido on his head, withers, and back for an 'exam'. This is difficult for the IG who has not been brought up in the breed ring or learning to 'stack'. Their tendency is to go forward toward the judge to assist them in any petting that may be solicited, or to become insecure at the approach of the judge, and run back to the handler! This exam is worth 30 points. The same heeling pattern is then repeated, minus the figure eight, but with the dog off leash. The Heel Free exercise is worth 40 points.

"Marilyn Langstaff of Georgia related this experience when she and Fara Shi'Ori, UD, were doing the heel free routine. They were at an outside show where there usually isn't much of a barrier between the dogs being judged and the spectators. Suddenly, a little boy ran out of the crowd, grabbed Fara and hugged her, put her down, and then ran off! Luckily, both Marilyn and Fara were able to regain their composure and complete the exercise!

"The Recall exercise is next. The handler leaves the dog in the sit-stay position and goes approximately thirty feet away. On the judge's command, the handler calls the dog in to sit in front of the handler, then directs the dog to return to the heel position on the handler's left side. This is the first time in the IG's show routine that they are put in an isolated position while the handler walks a good distance away. Then, with that bundled energy and need to return to their owner quickly, the speed coming in can sometimes be too fast to stop! Therefore stopping at the 'front' position sometimes can be a problem. Variations the IGs add for audience enjoyment and embarrassment of the handler are bouncing off the legs of the handler before sitting crooked, or running past the handler while trying to stop, then correcting and coming to front. The recall is worth 30 points. Thus far we have accounted for 140 of the 200 total points.

"Each dog has done these exercises individually up to this point. After a dozen or so dogs have completed the individuals, they are all brought back into the ring for the group exercises. The dogs are put in a row on a sit-stay, the handlers leave and walk across the ring to a distance of about thirty feet. They return to their dogs after one minute. Hopefully, all have held their sit-stay. Then on the judge's command, the dogs are told to lie down. The handlers again leave their dogs, and the dogs must hold the down-stay position for a total of three minutes. The group exercises are worth 30 points each. However, it is usually an all-or-none situation. The dog may get minor points deducted if they shift their body slightly for comfort, but if they break their stay position, not only do they lose the 30 points entirely, they have failed at the entire attempt to achieve a leg.

"The 'stays' are also difficult for the environmentally sensitive IG. If the climate is too cold (or too hot), their natural tendency is to break the sit-stay into a comfortable down position. Since the down is a very defenceless, submissive position, and since there is usually something 'big' on either side of them, muscles start to tense and their little elbows come up off the mat. When

Slone clearing the high jump with dumb-bell – U CDX Evergreen's Free Spirit Am. Can. CDX, TDI, CGC. Owned by Karen Langenbrunner.

Timothy King.

Pucci clearing the broad jump – Avagadro's One Puccini CDX, Can. CD, CGC. Owned by Betty Juergensmeyer.

Barb Zurawski.

those not-too-well padded joints hit the hard surfaces and are told to stay there, a training challenge presents itself!

"When Fido has completed these Novice exercises with the appropriate scoring, he receives a 'leg'. After three 'legs', the Kennel Club will award the title of Companion Dog, and Fido will be known formally as Fido, CD. Once Fido has earned his CD, he is eligible to enter the Open classes. Up to this point, an average of a year's worth of training and showing has been applied. The exercises in the Open Class become more difficult, and the dog needs to start working a little farther away from the owner. It is at this point that many IG trainers start running into difficulty. Insecurity starts to build as the exercises become more difficult.

"The heeling is first, but off the leash from the beginning, including a figure eight. A total of 40 points is possible for this Heel Free. The Recall is then done, but with a challenge. As the dog is coming in to the handler, on the judge's command, the dog is commanded to 'drop' – halt forward progression and lie down immediately. Once the dog is down, the judge tells the handler to call the dog on in for the completion of the exercise. Not only is there the problem of curbing that forward propulsion of the IG, but having them go into that horrid down position! Most IGs have at one time or another performed the 'squat on recall' to the amusement of the audience. The drop on recall exercise is worth 30 points.

"The next required exercise is definitely *not* an IG thing to do. A dumb-bell is introduced, made out of wood or a hard plastic, and fitted to the individual dog. Training an IG to put that (ugh!) *thing* in his mouth can definitely require some patience on the part of the trainer. The dumb-bell is thrown on command, the dog is sent to fetch on command, and then presents the dumb-bell at the 'front' before returning to heel position at the side.

"The Retrieve On Flat is worth 20 points. To increase the difficulty, the exercise is repeated, but this time the dumb-bell is thrown over a solid white hurdle, which the dog must jump over to retrieve the dumb-bell. The height of the jump is proportionate to the height of the dog. The retrieve over the high-jump is worth 30 points. The final individual exercise is the broad jump, testing the dog's ability to jump width instead of height. The width of the jump is again proportionate to the dog's height. To make this exercise unique, the handler leaves the dog facing the jump, then walks to the side of the jump before commanding the dog to jump it. The broad jump is worth 20 points. Since jumping definitely *is* an IG thing to do, the crowd is entertained by the IG jumping much higher and farther than needed!

"The group exercises are next, but the long sit is now for three minutes and the long down for five minutes. To make it more difficult, the entire group of handlers have left the ring and are out of sight. It is wonderful to see an entire group of dogs holding their position with no handlers around. The funniest sight I have seen during an Open group exercise was my dog Slone being placed next to an Irish Wolfhound! And once during training at one of our local classes, all of the Open handlers lined up our dogs, told them to sit-stay, and left the ring to hide behind an adjoining wall.

"My dog, Lace, was just learning to develop confidence during this exercise, but was still somewhat insecure. She got up, left the line of dogs, came and peeked around the corner to verify where I was, then went back and sat in line, although not in her original place! Who says these little guys can't think? Again three qualifying scores for three 'legs', and Fido now has his CDX, or Companion Dog Excellent title. Marian Webster of New Jersey owned the first IG Companion Dog AKC title holder, earned on 28th September 1952, called Mia Lisa of Geddensburg, who was also the first CDX dog, earning the title on 19th November 1953.

"Training a dog through a Utility (university) level is a grand achievement for anyone. The dog is now working mainly as an independent unit under the handler's direction. He must learn to think and act while away from his handler. The 40 point heeling pattern is now called the Signal Exercise. Not only is the dog off leash, but working under *no* verbal command from the handler. Only hand signals are permitted. At the end of the heeling pattern, the handler will stand the dog, leave him and walk across the ring, signal him to lie down, sit up, then come in and front, then finish to the handler's left side. All of this is done at the judge's signal, with only hand signals from the handler to their dog. Again, the dreaded 'elbows have to touch the mat', or drop, is incorporated.

"Next is the scent articles. Four leather and four metal dumb-bells, or articles, are touched by a steward and placed approximately twenty feet away from the team of dog and handler. Again as

Lace with correctly fitting utility article – U CDX Evergreen's Aery of Brandwin UD, Can. CDX, TDI, CGC. Owned by Karen Langenbrunner.

Lace clearing the bar jump – U CDX Evergreen's Aery of Brandwin UD, Can. CDX, TDI, CGC. Owned by Karen Langenbrunner.

Timothy King

with the dumb-bell, the articles must be fitted to the individual dog. The handler has a fifth leather and metal article that they rub with their bare hands in order to put their own scent on it. The judge will accept one of the scented articles from the handler, carry it to the group of articles scented by the steward and randomly place it among the others without touching it. At the judge's command, the team turns and the dog is sent to retrieve the one article the handler has scented. The exercise is then repeated with the second article the handler has scented. Each article is worth 30 points. The United Kennel Club only requires that the metal articles be used, but in Canada a third article made of wood is added.

"A Directed Retrieve glove exercise follows, worth 30 points. Lightweight, white cotton work-gloves are used. With the dog's back turned, a steward places three gloves approximately 20 feet behind the team: one glove is directly behind them, and one to each side, approximately ten feet apart. The judge tells the handler which specific glove to retrieve; the team must turn to face that glove, and the dog is sent to fetch it. The United Kennel Club requires two variations of the glove retrieve, and Canada offers a 'seek back', another variation using only one dark leather glove.

"The Moving Stand exercise is worth 30 points, which brings back the novice stand for exam, but with a little more difficulty. On command, the team heels forward. Again on command from the judge, the handler must tell the dog to stand-stay without halting their own forward movement. The handler walks to a distance of approximately ten feet away, turns and faces the dog. At this point, the judge will 'examine' the dog, but with two hands, more like a conformation examination. After the judge is finished, the dog is called directly to heel position instead of the usual sit in front.

"The last Utility exercise involves two extremes for the IG. A fun time jumping, but a difficult move going away from the handler. The team of dog and handler stand at one end of the ring. To their right, and approximately ten feet away, is either a solid white jump as was used in the Open level, or a black and white single bar jump, which is much harder to see, and could give Fido the opportunity to go under instead of over it. The other jump is placed to the team's left, approximately twenty feet from the first jump. The dog is sent *away* from the handler, straight down the middle of the ring, between the two jumps. The dog must go at least ten feet past the jumps. The handler calls the dog's name, and has Fido turn to face the handler and sit.

"The judge then tells the handler which obstacle the dog should jump. With an outstretched hand toward the correct jump and a verbal command, the handler sends the dog over the jump. After the front and finish, the entire exercise is repeated over the opposite jump. The whole two-jump exercise is worth 40 points. After three qualifying scores, the coveted title of Utility Dog is earned! Theoretically, there could be ten Golden Retrievers, Shetland Sheepdogs, or Border Collies at any one trial to finish this third Utility leg. Since the first IG earned an AKC Companion Dog title, there have been only eleven IG UD titles earned. These dogs and handlers deserve to be individually recognised:

OBEDIENCE TITLE HOLDERS
1. Vittorio Torino Di Finstock, UD. Owned by E. & R. Reed. Earned on November 22nd 1964.
2. Fara Shi'Ori, UD. Owned by Marilyn Langstaff. Earned on September 24th 1972.
3. Ch. Ser Jeno Mio Bambino, UD. Owned by Marian Hammell. Earned on December 4th 1977.
4. Ch. Il Abbadonato Bandito, UD. Owned by Marian Hammell. Earned on November 11th 1979.
5. Ch. Majana's Nicolina Di Lucia, UD. Owned by A. Zniewski & E. Connolly. Earned on May 5th 1984.
6. Karma's Mario, UD. Owned by E. Anderson. Earned on July 14th 1984.
7. Colacove Daydreamer, UDT. Owned by Karen Froemming. Earned on September 6th 1987.
8. Ch. Mira Mumble T Peg, UD. Owned by Teri Dickinson. Earned on July 9th 1989.
9. Sooper Dooper Cooper, UD. Owned by Karen Covill. Earned on July 14th 1990.
10. Ch. Bandilane Summer's Magpie, UD. Owned by Joan Pronto. Earned on November 11th 1990.
11. U-CDX Evergreen's Aery of Branduin, UD, Can.CDX. Owned by Ken and Karen Langenbrunner. Earned on March 14th 1992.

"Tracking is another sport which is popular in the United States and Canada. The main object

Colacove Day Dreamer: the first and only IG to earn a Utility Dog title and a Tracking title. He is pictured straining into his tracking harness as he indicates the trail scent.

of this sport is for the dog to use his nose and follow a track laid by someone 30 to 120 minutes earlier. In other words, follow where the first person walked. The track must be at least 440 yards long and have three to five turns to it. At the end, the dog must indicate an object dropped by the person who laid the track. The dog works on a harness and on a long line, at least 20 feet ahead of the handler. Since so much land is needed to run a tracking test, approximately 5 acres per dog, a dog must be certified before it actually enters a test. To be certified, the handler must actually work a dog through a track to show that the dog can do it. Once a dog has passed one tracking test, a TD (Tracking Dog) title can be added to its name.

"To achieve the next difficult level for a TDX (Tracking Dog Excellent), the track must be three to five hours old, it must have have five to seven turns in it, it must be a minimum length of 800 yards, and have a different person cross over where the first person walked not once, but twice, for a cross track. If you are picturing a nice grassy meadow for tracking, you're wrong! It can be through thickets, woods, mud, blackberry patches, and even over a fence. And the TDX terrain would be a little harder yet, crossing paved roads and water. To date, there are four IG TDs, and they also deserve to be individually recognised:

1. Colacove Daydreamer, UDT. Owner Karen Froemming. Earned on October 12th 1980.
2. Ch. Etter's Roman Prize of Silk, TD. Owned by Judy M. West. Earned on June 3rd 1984.
3. Elwig Cowboy Joe, TD. Owned by M. Cornell. Earned on July 10th 1984.
4. Banjo's Diamond in the Rough, TD. Owned by Barbara and John Horn. Earned May 2nd 1989.

Marguerite O'Donnell, based in Quebec, highlights the Obedience scene in Canada and pays particular tribute to a very special little Italian Greyhound:

"Dog Obedience Competition in Canada is a very popular sport and growing from year to year. It attracts people of all ages and from all walks of life. There never have been many Italian Greyhounds competing, but in my opinion they can be a very interesting breed to train, with the added advantage that jumping presents no problem. What they do not view with any enthusiasm are wet and cold weather, long wet grass and cold rubber mats for the long sit and down exercises. The exercises in Canada are very similar to those performed in the United States with a few slight differences. In the Novice Class the stand for examination in Canada is done on leash; the high jump is the height of the dog at the withers in Open Class, and in Utility (the highest class) we have the seek back, in which the handler sends his dog back to find and return a glove which has been dropped during an intricate heeling pattern, whereas in the United States this exercise has been replaced by the Directed Retrieve.

"It is not every day that one sees Italian Greyhounds in Obedience. I believe that my own Can. Ch. Sirham Sonatina, UD competing in the sixties, was the first Italian Greyhound to compete in Obedience in Canada. However, an Italian Greyhound that I would especially like to mention is Ch. Piacere Carry on Damn Yankee, belonging to Miss J. Nelson. This little hound achieved fame by winning High in trial on two consecutive days, with scores of 196 and 194.05 from the Novice B class on June 9th and 10th 1989. From Western Canada we have a Ch. Laba Dawn Allegro, CD, Ch. Salswifts Cyano d'Broomhall, Ch. Broomhall's Dolce Sophia, CD, and, of course, Pam Heap and her dogs, who returned to the UK.

"I have always admired sight hounds, but it was when I saw Ch. Flaminia of Alpine (7/62) win the Toy Group at the Westminster Show in New York that I became infatuated with the Italian Greyhound, and since then I have never considered acquiring another breed. In the course of time I made enquiries and saw a number of Italian Greyhounds, but when I met Sirham Sonatina, a solid blue puppy, bred by Audrey Benbow, then I really lost my heart. I brought her home to live with a Weimaraner, a German Shepherd and two cats. Tina, as we called her, never thought of herself as a delicate little dog but shared our long walks in the woods with Charles Augustus, the Weimaraner, and Flash, the German Shepherd. On the weekends, we would often walk all day long in the beautiful autumn weather, rarely meeting anyone, but often seeing tracks of moose, deer and bear.

"When she was old enough I started showing her in Conformation and training her in Obedience. She won her Novice Obedience title in 1968, and she finished her Championship at the same show on the same afternoon as she won her first Leg in CDX in 1969. She won her UD title in 1971 and she also won a High in Trial in CDX and a High in Class in Utility, defeating a large class of Standard Poodles and German Shepherds. She had a wonderfully stable temperament and always gave me all her attention. On one occasion in Conformation we came up against an Italian Greyhound who had been doing a lot of winning but had rather shaky nerves. The judge had trouble making up his mind and asked us to put both dogs up on the table for a final going over. I had also been showing my Weimaraner in the Sporting Group, where at that time the examination was done with leash removed. I set Tina up on the table, took off her leash and stepped back, leaving her as motionless and elegant as a little Renaissance statue. The judge decided in Tina's favour.

"We won two 'legs' on CDX without too much difficulty and then problems arose. Tina at a

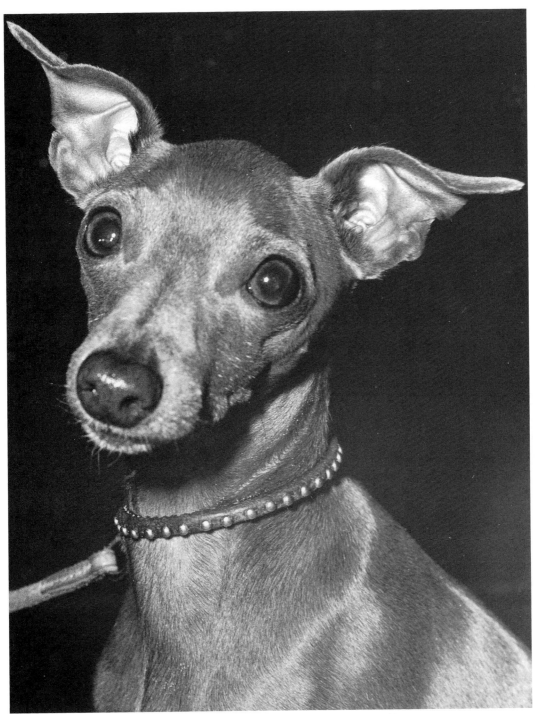

Tina – Ch. Sirham Sonatina UD – owned by Marguerite O'Donnell.

trial had to jump into direct blinding sunlight. The high jump was poorly set up, she brushed it and it all fell down on her, giving her quite a shock. It took some little time to retrain her but the day came when I thought that she was ready for that final leg. I promised her a filet mignon if she passed! Pass she did, with a High in Trial. When I took her up to claim the award, she sensed my pleasure in her performance and celebrated by running madly in circles of joy when the judge handed me the medal which we had won. I kept my word and she had a whole filet mignon just for herself.

"Another time when I was showing her in CDX the board floor was laid over the ice in a hockey rink. When she jumped the broad jump, on landing one hind leg went completely through between the boards and she was firmly pinned there. I was terrified that she would struggle and break her leg. One quick command "Stay" and she waited motionless until she was freed by the judge and ring stewards, who managed to prise the boards apart. Many years later, when she was no longer competing and I had her with me at a show, a man came up to me and said 'Isn't that the little dog that went through the boards at the hockey arena in Ottawa?' When I replied 'Yes', he smiled and said 'I've never forgotten her. I was the judge.'

"I don't remember her ever making a mistake in Scent Discrimination or breaking a long stay, but she also had other important qualities. She was a wonderful therapy dog, long before therapy dogs were in vogue. On one occasion we visited a retirement home and before going from room to room to visit the patients confined to their beds, we put on a little demonstration of Utility Obedience in the rather small living room, crowded with enthusiastic inmates. At the moment that I sent her out for the scent articles (dumb-bells) two dear old ladies thought that they would show their appreciation by scattering chocolates and peppermints in profusion amongst the articles. My hair fairly stood on end, but Tina made her way through the goodies as best she could and brought back the correct articles, first the wood, then the leather and then the metal, these being the ones that had my scent on them, among the twelve scattered dumb-bells.

"She was in great demand for Junior Handling and in later years young people would come up to me and say 'Do you remember you lent me Tina to show when I was just starting out?' Many a school and playground she visited; she loved children, and when off leash would often cross the street to talk to them. She would serve as a model when I talked to children about how to approach and treat dogs. She never gave me a moment's anxiety. As she grew older she loved to lie on the sofa, opposite the chair where I sat to read. I tried to avoid eye contact with her because, if our eyes met, she would very laboriously get down and cross the room to put a paw on my arm and give me a kiss. Tina was fifteen when she left me to join Flash and Charles on the moose and bear trails in the Happy Hunting Grounds.

"Although I have written this as a tribute to a very special dog, don't think of the Italian Greyhound as a dog only to grace a sofa or share a bed. I have trained others up to CDX level. One who is my close companion at the present time is, in the words of a well known judge, one of the happiest, the most confident and fastest scent discrimination workers that he had ever seen. It was with great sadness that I had to withdraw her from competition because of a heart condition. However, she can still perform 'good works' and visits one of our local treatment clinics and homes for the retired on a regular basis.

"Italian Greyhounds are sensitive, but there seems to be no limit to what they can learn. In the United States there is even one with a tracking degree and I have been told that they have also been used to detect drugs at airports. So you see how versatile the Italian Greyhound can be – a combination of beauty, great charm and intelligence."

OBEDIENCE ITALIAN GREYHOUNDS IN ALBERTA:

Ch. Laba Dawn Allegro CD (F) (Canada), callname 'Fizzy'.
Regd # TL577883, born June 8th 1986.
(Ch. Pascal Il Piccolo Azzuro – Ch. Mai Blumes Tinkerbell).
Bred by F. L. & B. A. Allewell. Owned and trained by Mrs L. Jean MacDonald, Edmonton.
Earned her CD on June 11th 1988.
Was trained to CDX and failed three Trials before retiring to a pet home.

Ch. Salswift's Cyano d'Broomhall CD (M) (USA), callname 'Cy'.
Regd # 1026059, born January 29th 1988.
(Can. Am. Ch. Salswift's Skyrocket d'Dasa – Can. Am. Ch. Tomaso's Spitfire d'Salswift).
Bred by Sally Smyth. Imported by Donald Brown but later owned and trained by Ms Tracy Therens, Calgary.
Earned his CD on August 5th 1989.
Never trained to CDX but did appear in 'Superdog Show' at Calgary Stampede.

Ch. Broomhall's Dolce Sophia CD (F) (Can), callname 'Sophie'.
Regd # XA829023, born January 20th 1990.
(Ch. Turigner Gold Run, Imp. UK – Ch. Piacere's Tresca d'Broomhall).
Bred by Donald W. Brown. Owned and trained by Ms Janet Yee, Calgary.
Earned her CD November 30th 1991. Will be trained to CDX

Geoka's Clio of Broomhall (F) (Canada), callname 'Clio'.
Regd # TN579185, born July 10th 1986.
(Can. Am. Ch. Gogi's Bronze Buckwheat – Gogi's Blue Gene Babe).
Bred by Kathy Ralph. Owned and trained by Donald W. Brown.
Clio competed in two trials – one failure and one score of 195 – before taking time out to have a litter.

Betty McHugh from Oshawa, Ontario, has kindly compiled the following Obedience statistics from Canada from 1966:

	CD	CDX	UD
1968	1		
1969		1	
1971			1
1975	1		
1978	3	1	1
1987	3		
1988	1		
1989	5	1	

I should point out that Obedience in the UK and USA have different requirements. In the UK Obedience and Working Trials have a totally different set of regulations. In brief, Obedience classes in the UK consist of Pre-Beginners, Beginners, Novice, Class A, Class B and Class C. The tests cover Heel on Lead, Heel Free, Recall, Retrieve a Dumb-bell/article, Stays and Scent Discrimination. As for Working Trials, there are Open and Championship Trials. Under the latter heading the following qualifications can be awarded: Companion Dog (CD), Utility Dog (UD), Working Dog (WD), Tracking Dog (TD), Patrol Dog (PD).

Chapter Eleven

THE VERSATILE ITALIAN GREYHOUND

Some owners have had the opportunity to accompany their dogs on excursions into the world of fashion modelling, television and films. Glamorous as this may sound, in fact the other side of the camera is a lot of hard work. My own experiences have been with Ch. Patchwork Of Dairylane, who was asked by *Vogue* magazine to feature in a full double-page colour spread to form what was to be a Renaissance style of picture. David Montgomery, a photographer from the USA, was in charge, and we dutifully travelled one very hot summer's day to the studio in London. The other live characters taking part were a white fluffy cat and a small toddler, who was dressed in a white dress from a very expensive boutique.

The set was full of wonderful antiques that had been acquired from various famous stores, and the backcloth was a superb tapestry. Patches, who is white with a couple of fawn patches, was to wear a blue ribbon around her neck, and the little girl's dress had the same blue ribbon on it. There was a beautiful large carved chair, a large marble-topped table, and in one corner there was an enormous arrangement of fruit and flowers. The set, complete with imitation white pillars, looked wonderful, but trying to put the three 'characters' into place was not to prove so easy. The cat hated all and sundry and hissed continuously, the little girl was only tiny, and had to be coaxed with chocolate to co-operate; only Patches was as good as gold, sometimes standing and sometimes sitting on her blue cushion. By the end of the morning we were getting nowhere fast, the child's dress was covered in chocolate, so was the beautifully tiled floor, and the photographer was swearing that he would never work with children again – it was time to take a break for lunch.

The chocolate was removed from the dress and the floor, and the child was found a quiet spot to have a sleep. Patches used the time to have a cuddle with everybody, and won the hearts of the technicians and staff – as well as some of the food from their plates. After the lunch break we started again, and I was commissioned not only to tell Patches what she was to do, but also to take charge of the little girl, whose mother was asked to keep away! I was positioned with my back flattened to the side of the set, keeping out of the range of the photographer while talking to the little girl and to Patches. Finally, late afternoon, it was 'in the can'. The published version looked really gorgeous, and despite all the hard work, it was a fascinating experience. Patches

Mrs Sue Dunning with Harry – Anjuskar Lorenzo – perfecting the 'hoopla' for his part in the BBC TV serial Alfonso Bonzo.

also appeared on television in the Pedigree Chum commercial after winning Best of Breed at Crufts in 1983.

Susan Pinkus, who lives in New Jersey, USA, has also had experience of chaperoning her dogs in a modelling session when she took nine IGs to the Italian *Vogue* magazine for some photos by Bill King in their Manhattan studio. The dogs took to their new role with the lovely models immediately, and did not bat an eye when fans were used to blow the model's hair, and strobe lights were flashing like lightning. Controlling nine dogs is never easy, and Susan had to unravel all the leads while make-up and hair were adjusted on the models. Hundreds of photos were taken to get enough material for the four pages required, proving once again what patient and amenable little dogs Italian Greyhounds can be. Another pair of IGs who recently appeared as fashion models were Ch. Cenere La Traviata Of Caccia and Ch. Cenere Il Turco At Caccia, both belonging to Linnet Loh. Her daughter Vivien was one of several other handlers with Italian breeds invited to accompany their charges to Harrods, the big department store in London, to model Burberry dog coats. Famous for their human clothing, the manufacturers were branching out to extend their range to the pets of their customers. Once again the dogs behaved impeccably even when posing with Neopolitan Mastiffs. However, their owner did decline to remove their leads, as was suggested to make the pose more natural!

I was approached by an animal casting company who wanted some Italians to take part in a

An IG makes an ideal therapy dog.

children's television serial being made for the BBC. The dogs would have to be fairly biddable as they would be requested to jump up into someone's arms on command. Most IGs are quite happy to jump up, but on command is a different matter. I put the casting company in touch with Sue Dunning, who is currently one of the very few IG owners in the UK who does regular Obedience training with her dogs. The script required that the dog would be surrounded by lots of children, and a 'recall' would be needed. Sue took two dogs because, while Harry (Anjuskar Lorenzo) was a little reluctant to perform some of the stunts, Freddie (Philtre Federigo) had no such qualms. Hector (Anjuskar Luigi) did not want to jump into anyone's arms, so the first two were booked. In fact, the IG in the story was a bitch by the name of Giulietta, so this 'defect' was overcome by the dogs wearing smart little red coats, trimmed with gold, to hide the evidence!

The serial was called *Alfonso Bonzo* and all IG enthusiasts watched it avidly. The dogs were brilliant. Sue had to take them for rehearsals at the BBC, and then the action took place at a school in London. Harry jumped into the arms of the actress playing the part of the teacher, which he was supposed to do each time he heard the words 'Giulietta Hoopla'. Freddie had to run through a hall full of children and on to a stage with dancing children, which never bothered him one little bit. He had two hours to learn to ride in a basket on the front of a bicycle and he had to be chased through a concrete tunnel by the supposed Headmaster, and then sit and refuse to play with him. Here his Obedience training was invaluable as the Headmaster was supposed to try and persuade him to get up. As long as the dogs could see Sue they co-operated beautifully, so she had to bob about under cameras so that she could keep in their view and thus make them obey the commands. The series was a great success and there is talk of a sequel.

Although we all appreciate how much comfort can be achieved from loving our four-footed friends, it is now being realised that many can benefit from this, even if they do not own dogs themselves. Therapy dogs, known as PAT dogs in the UK, are now becoming widely recognised for the important work they do in hospitals and other residential homes. There is a wonderful chemistry that exists between people and dogs, and this has proved invaluable in caring for the sick and the elderly. There are also cases reported of patients who are mentally ill and very withdrawn, but who will talk to a dog. Some years ago I sold a pair of IG litter sisters to a charming couple who had a son suffering from Downs Syndrome. They had two older children, but the young boy of about fifteen hardly ever spoke to anyone. However, they discovered that he would sit on the sofa with a little dog cuddled up on each side and 'talk' to them, in a way he could never relate with his human family.

Sue Dunning has three of her Italians registered with the PAT organisation in the UK. They are Hector (Anjuskar Luigi), Harry (Anjuskar Lorenzo) and Kelly (Anjuskar Midas Madonna), and they were all assessed by a vet or a trainer for fitness and suitability of temperament. Many people assume that only larger fluffy dogs will make good candidates for this task, but in fact some people are overcome by large dogs and with anyone a little frail or insecure a small Italian is light enough to sit on a lap quite easily. The IGs love to be cuddled, and as they do not shed hair like so many breeds, this is another asset. There is another organisation that uses dogs to be 'the ears' for deaf people, indicating when the doorbell rings or the telephone, etc. The idea is fast gaining ground, proving that dogs can serve a dual role, as indeed they already do as Guide Dogs.

Chapter Twelve

THE ITALIAN GREYHOUND IN ART AND ANECDOTE

The beautiful, graceful Italian Greyhound has inspired artists from earliest times, and the breed has been depicted in marble, bronze, pottery and tapestry, as well as in numerous paintings. For many IG owners, this is an added attraction of the breed, and IG enthusiasts spend much time tracking down works of art which feature Italian Greyhounds in museums, art galleries and stately homes, or on the lookout for an IG collectable that might be buried in an antique shop. Some of the collections actually list paintings which feature certain breeds of dog, and the Scottish National Portrait Gallery, for example, has a very detailed index of paintings of 'Greyhound'-type dogs with several actually recorded as Italian Greyhounds. Obviously, not everybody can afford to buy a major work of art, but looking at paintings, and the opportunity to purchase colour postcards of them, is within everyone's reach.

Italian Greyhounds appeared in many Renaissance paintings, and so IG owners regularly scour the Christmas card selections to see if any have IGs in the scene. Gerard David (c.1460-1523) used the little dogs in several of his paintings: *The Martyrdom of St Ursula* and *Le Jugement de Cambyse* in the Bruges Museum, and *The Virgin and Child with Saints and Donor* in the National Gallery in London. In this last picture the Virgin Mary takes the centre of the painting with the Baby on her lap, and the little fawn Italian Greyhound is sitting on the mosaic floor in front of her. *The Adoration of the Magi* is the title to paintings by Hieronymus Bosch (c.1450-1516), Sasetta (1392-1450) and Hans Memling (1430-1495). There is a very colourful painting called *A Winter Feast,* which is a detail from an illuminated page in the calendar of the *Tres Riches Heures* of the Duke of Berry (1416) in the Musee Conde, Chantilly. This shows a food-laden table with the courtiers about to eat, and in the forefront is a white IG being approached by one of the gentlemen. All of these have been reproduced on Christmas cards at different times and this is a very inexpensive way of adding to a collection of memorabilia. The lovely tapestries of the *Lady and the Unicorn,* housed in the Museum of Paris, are available as a set of six postcards. The two main characters are accompanied by rabbits, birds, flowers and Italian Greyhounds on a red background. They depict the five senses – smell, sight, taste, touch and hearing, and 'A Mon Seul Desir'.

Visitors to the Vatican in Rome will see many wonderful Roman statues depicting small hounds. The British Museum in London also houses a fine group of similar figures in the Roman Sculpture Gallery in the Department of Greek and Roman Antiquities, which were found in the 18th century at Lanuvium, a town which is on the Via Appia, south-east of Rome. The sculptures are made of marble and certainly give the impression of being Italian Greyhounds. One pair of hounds is depicted sucking each other's ears, a habit well known to all IG owners. The museum is reluctant to classify these dogs as a particular breed because, while there are many written references to dogs and hounds in Greek and Latin sources, and innumerable representations in Classical Art, the concept of a breed in our strict sense was unknown.

Throughout history a number of famous personalities have been reputed to own Italian Greyhounds, and there are numerous anecdotes which make the breed's history even more colourful. For example: did Cleopatra really take an Italian Greyhound to Rome as a gift for Caesar, wrapped in the rug from which she appeared? It is hard to disentangle fact from legend, but certainly in the painting by William Blake (1757-1827) called *Sir Geoffrey Chaucer and the Nine and Twenty Pilgrims on their Journey to Canterbury*, which hangs in the Stirling Maxwell Collection, Pollock House, Glasgow, UK, the "small houndes" running alongside the Prioress look like Italian Greyhounds. Blake also made an engraving of this and it can be seen at the Yale Centre for British Art in the Paul Mellon Collection in the USA.

Most wealthy households throughout Europe had hounds of varying sizes, and the small Italian Greyhounds were considered such a prize that it is natural they would appear in so many paintings. It is thought this may be why the breed appears so frequently in the religious paintings that were commissioned by Italian noblemen – not because they normally accompanied the lowly shepherds, tending flocks, but because they were the beloved animals of their patrons and they liked to see them adorn the paintings in this way. Several of the dogs depicted in these paintings actually wear collars that have coats of arms on them. Bernardo Visconti, living in the 15th century, was reputed to have 5000 dogs for hunting, and the ordinary people were expected to feed them and look after them.

The Este family was also famous for their dogs and they are referred to in very early manuscripts still in existence in Florence. The Medici family are also reputed to have kept a number of the breed. It has to be assumed that it was because of the breed's particular popularity and its appearance in so many Italian works of art that it became known as the 'Italian Greyhound', even if, in the very beginning, their first home was Egypt.

In the *Illustrated London News*, June 2nd 1956, a story appeared concerning Queen Her-Neit's tomb in Egypt of 5000 years ago, her jewels and her pet dog. This was considered a unique architectural discovery by Professor Walter B. Emery Edwards, Professor of Egyptology in the University of London and Director of the excavations. A picture of the remains of a dog are depicted, which could easily be a small hound of Italian Greyhound type. To quote from the article:

"The 5000 year old tomb of Queen Her-Neit, is outstanding in interest even among the Royal tombs of the archaic necropolis at North Sakkara. Its large superstructure is exceptionally well preserved, so much so that the Egyptian Government has decided to restore it and partly cover it to preserve it. Its architectural construction is a unique combination of two grave forms – the domed burial pit of Upper Egypt and the brick mastaba of Lower Egypt.

"Further, the actual burial chamber, though looted in antiquity, is well preserved and has yielded a number of interesting objects, some of which we illustrate, and in particular a gold and carnelian necklace which is quite outstanding for the period. Several of the tombs in the necropolis have been surrounded with a number of subsidiary burials, presumably those of servants who had died, probably by taking poison, in order to accompany their master into the Next World. Queen Her-Neit had only one companion for her journey after death: her pet dog, a Saluki-like animal, whose curled up skeleton was found buried just outside the entrance to her tomb."

As the homes of noblemen throughout the world became more luxurious, exotic gifts were exchanged by travellers and courtiers in Royal circles and these included cloth, jewels, and spices, but it is quite likely that Italian Greyhounds sometimes formed part of the transactions. It has been said that King Henry VIII of England had a number of IGs and sent some as gifts to the Queen of France. There is also an amusing tale that when Henry VIII sent a representative to see the Pope in Rome about his divorce from Catherine of Aragon, the English courtier had an Italian Greyhound in his arms. No one knows whether it was intended as a gift, or whether it was the courtier's personal companion, but we are told that when the Pope put his foot forward for the visitor to kiss, as is the practice, the little dog flew at the eminent gentleman, thinking it was a move against his master!

Anne Boleyn, who eventually became the second of Henry's six wives, had a pet spaniel called 'Little Purkoy' and an Italian Greyhound by the name of 'Urien'. It seems Urien was being presented to the Queen as a gift from a courtier, when she snatched the dog from him before he could finish his formal introductory speech because she thought it was so beautiful. Royal Doulton have produced a figurine of Anne with her two pets.

From the information available it would seem that 'all things Italian' were popular during the reign of Queen Elizabeth I – music, poetry and clothes. There are no paintings of the Queen with an Italian Greyhound. However, there is a painting of her half-sister, Mary Queen Of Scots, called *Condemnation to death of Mary Stuart*, that shows two Italian Greyhounds in the foreground. At one time this was in the home of the Duke and Duchess of Devonshire, but it is now in private hands. During the reign of the Stuarts there is much evidence of Italian Greyhounds, who are depicted playing a prominent role in paintings of family groups. The most famous one of all is *A La Chasse*, which is of Queen Anne of Denmark, consort of James I of England and VI of Scotland. This is the property of Her Majesty Queen Elizabeth II and was painted by Van Somer. In the painting Queen Anne is about to mount her horse and has a servant behind her. There are five Italian Greyhounds at the foot of her skirts, some fawn, others blue, and blue and white. They give the impression they are about to accompany their mistress, and they vary slightly in size from possibly 8 to 16lb. They wear collars with their mistress's coat of arms. In the background of the picture is her home, called Oatlands. The Queen was supposed to have preferred pictures to people, and possibly she found dogs more companionable, guessing from the number she appeared to own. This picture could be seen at one time at Hampton Court; however, it is not currently on view to the public. I understand it is now part of the Royal Collection at St. James's Palace, London.

Queen Henrietta Maria, wife of Charles I (1625-beheaded 1649) was the daughter of Henry IV of France, and there are several enchanting portraits of the family with their dogs. Painted by Vermeer (1632-75) of the Van Dyck school, examples can be found in the Birmingham City Museum, UK. The Wallace Collection in London also boasts paintings by Gonzales Coques (1614-84) of family groups accompanied by their little hounds. Coques was Flemish and a popular portrait artist in the Van Dyck style. In the Fredricksborg Castle in Denmark two lovely paintings include Italian Greyhounds. One shows the castle in the background, and the centre of

'The Marlborough Family' by
Sir Joshua Reynolds.
Reproduced by kind permission
of His Grace the Duke of
Marlborough. Located in the
Red Drawing Room, Blenheim
Palace.

Frederick the Great and his
Italian Greyhounds. Bronze
1821 by Gottfried Schadow.
Reproduced by kind
permission of Verband fur
das Deutsche Hundewesen
(VDH) Germany.

attention is a nobleman dressed in black and gold on a black horse (c. 1600). He has his attendants and a page and there are two dogs. The other shows Horsholm Castle in the background and is of Ulrik C. Gyldenloue, King Christian's son, and his wife Charlotte Amalie Krabbe (c 1700). There are two Italian Greyhounds – one is very tiny – and the lady is accompanied by three other ladies at a table, laden with fruit.

Sir Joshua Reynolds (1723-92) painted many noble families of his day, and a number of them have an Italian Greyhound in their company. One of his paintings is at Blenheim Palace, the home of the Duke of Marlborough, and this shows the 4th Duke with his family, which included six children, two King Charles Spaniels and a blue or black and white pied Italian Greyhound. It is well worth visiting the Red Drawing Room, Blenheim Palace, UK, where it hangs. The Birmingham City Museum has another painting by Reynolds, showing the Roffey family with their Italian Greyhound. The families portrayed are lavishly gowned, obviously looking their finest; the dogs must have been an important part of their lifestyle to be included in the family portrait.

There is often confusion between Italian Greyhound and Whippet owners as to which breed was owned by Frederick the Great of Prussia. I think the problem is that, as in many households of the period, the same Christian name is used and people get confused as to which Frederick is being referred to. In researching my own family history I discovered this, and it is very annoying to find how many times the eldest son had his father's name! Frederick the Great of Prussia – Frederick II (1712-1786) – was the son of the King of Prussia, Frederick William I. There were no Whippets at this time, and the marvellous statue of Frederick with two of his little dogs clearly shows them as examples of Italian Greyhounds. This was made of bronze in 1821 by Gottfried Schadow and is 90 cms high. It is to be found at Sans Souci, home of Frederick.

The younger Frederick loved music and played the flute and appreciated all things of beauty, and this was reflected in his choice of dogs as companions. It seems he kept them in large numbers, as many as thirty or so, and each had their individual names. Probably Biche is the best known, but there were also Diana, Pan, Pax, Amoretto, amongst others. Biche was always at his side, even at night, when the others were sent to their own quarters. It seems the dogs also had their own carriage so that when Frederick travelled they could accompany their master in appropriately fine style.

Legend has it that during a battle, the King was separated from his troops and when a Hungarian platoon came by he had to hide under a bridge to avoid discovery. Biche was instructed not to make a sound, and they hid in the ditch with the little dog curled up in her master's cloak, allowing the enemy to pass without a sound to betray them. Frederick later made a great fuss of her in front of his men and acclaimed her his most devout friend. It then seems Biche was captured in another battle and taken as hostage. The King was distraught, but eventually the little dog was returned to him once again.

It seems when she died Biche was given a monument of her own in the grounds of the home of Frederick at Sans Souci. It also seems that Frederick's greatest wish was that when he died he should be buried at Sans Souci alongside his dogs, but this did not happen as it was not considered grand enough for such an important Emperor. However, in 1991, the authorities eventually returned the remains of Frederick to the burial place of his choice – although the newspapers in the UK reported that he was being returned to his Whippets, causing much annoyance to the iG owners!

I, personally, think the confusion with the Fredericks has come about because a later descendant, namely Frederick III, who was Emperor in 1888, also owned small hounds. In fact, in the *Ladies' Kennel Journal*, dated 1896, a contributor, writing about the various dogs owned by Queen Victoria (1837-1901) refers to some Russian Greyhounds that were given to her by the Emperor of Russia and goes on to say:

"Not less interesting are the two smaller Greyhounds – Whippets in size, but not quite in lines – called Dainty and Bische, of which we also give portraits. Dainty was blue with white on chest, his mate all fawn. They belonged to the Emperor Frederick, and after his death were sent by the Empress to Windsor, where they died only a year or two ago. Though there is no trace of the breed now – except in Landseer's portraits of them – the Italian Greyhound was at one time a favourite dog with both Her Majesty and Prince Albert, and an authority on the subject says: 'I have seen a great many Italian Greyhounds, and some of the best I ever saw belonged to the Queen.'"

Queen Victoria had a great passion for dogs of all breeds. Some were kept indoors, but she also had many others that were housed in kennels built by Henry Ashton in the early 1840s. At this time there are records of thirty-two dogs in the kennels including Russian, English and Italian Greyhounds. Her first kennel man was not a success, but in 1848 Mr John Macdonald, known as Jager, came from Balmoral, Scotland, with his wife and children to take charge. In fact, Mrs Macdonald often took charge when her husband was absent.

A visitor to Windsor in 1854 wrote: "Mrs Macdonald let us in to pass through a succession of yards, where the different dogs were either together or separate, according as they liked each other's company. There were beautiful dogs of all kinds. The dogs were pleased to be noticed, and I should have liked to have sat down amongst them, and tried to draw them – the places were as sweet and clean as your chicken yards....".

The Queen's husband, Prince Albert, shared this love of dogs and he encouraged the Queen to assemble an album of portraits of their pets which is now kept in the Royal Library at Windsor Castle. Many of the paintings are by Friedrich Wilhelm Keyl (1823-71), a native of Frankfurt. Evidently Keyl came to England in 1845 to study with Sir Edwin Landseer. There is a picture by him called *Tiny, Nino, Fermach and Minka at the Kennels*. Tiny and Nino are two Italian Greyhounds, Minka and Fermach are fawn pugs. Tiny is fawn and Nino is white with fawn markings. Their heads come as high as the edge of the seat of the plush-covered, carved chair behind them. They appear a little round in skull but otherwise would compare well with today's dogs. There is often a question raised as to whether the well known dog, Eos, who belonged to Prince Albert, was an Italian Greyhound or not. In fact, she was a Greyhound, and she is depicted in marble at the feet of her master in his tomb in the Memorial Chapel at Windsor.

There is a painting in the Royal Household called *Eos and her Pups, Timor and Mishka*, by G. Morley. Landseer also painted her, and she is portayed standing in front of a table covered with a red cloth, edged with gold braiding, waiting by her master's black top hat and white gloves, which are on a footstool. She is a beautiful shape and has a shining black coat with white feet and chest. Register of the Royal dogs apparently recorded the birth of Eos from Greyhound stock. She originated from Coburg and was brought over by the Prince at the time of his marriage.

Mary Princess Royal, a great granddaughter of Queen Victoria, owned an Italian Greyhound and she was photographed with her dog Mosca in 1913. I have yet to track down the breeding of this dog – which was not a particularly small specimen – as there were several ladies of social standing who were breeding Italians at the time, and not all would have been registered with the

Kennel Club. Mr and Mrs Morgan (Nagrom) also sent an Italian Greyhound called Nagrom Conte to France to Her Grace The Duchess of Windsor in late l966. He was a male born in March l965 by Ch. Estrada Hermes out of Nagrom Bertuccio.

The Duchess, previously known as Mrs Wallis Simpson, an American lady, married Edward VIII after his abdication from the British throne in 1936. Their home in exile in the Bois de Boulogne, Paris, has been completely restored just as it was in their day by the present owner Mr Mohammed Al Fayed and is a private museum. A friend who has pugs, which were the breed always associated with the couple, has recently had the good fortune to visit the mansion. I understand it has a marvellous collection of pug furniture, cushions, firedogs and an incredible assortment of l8th and l9th century porcelain pugs.

In l985 I began to research the founding of the Italian Greyhound Club in Britain, and I opened up a veritable treasure of anecdotes about the people involved. The present Lord Abinger remembered his grandmother (Mrs Scarlett) always being surrounded by her Italian Greyhounds, and also recalled the fact that they always took over the best chairs! He also said Helen, Lady Abinger, was very much an animal-lover. Before her marriage to William Frederick Scarlett, she was known as Helen Magruder, and she met her future husband while he was stationed with his Regiment of the Scots Fusilier Guards near her home in Montreal, Canada. The third Baron Abinger, as he was, took his young wife back to Abinger Hall in Sussex. They eventually decided to sell the Hall and build a more lavish home in Scotland, to be known as Inverlochy Castle, where they brought up their three daughters and one son. This Castle is now an hotel. Queen Victoria spent a week at Inverlochy and wrote in her diary: "I never saw a lovelier or a more romantic spot."

The fourth Baron Abinger was involved with his mother in the formation of the Breed Club, and as he died young and unmarried, the title then passed to Capt. S. Leopold L. Scarlett of Boscombe Manor, Bournemouth, who was the eldest son of Mrs Bessie Florence Scarlett, who by this time was a widow. She had seven children herself, so was a busy lady with her dogs as well. Mrs Scarlett, as already stated, was brought up by the only surviving son of the poet Percy Bysshe Shelley (1792-1822) who lived for a time in Italy. Sir Percy seems to have been the one who first introduced her to Italian Greyhounds. An associate of Sir Percy Florence Shelley, the Hon. Grantley Berkeley wrote in his book *From My Life & Recollections:*

"At this moment one of the prettiest little Italian Greyhounds I ever saw, by name Linda, in the possession of Lady Shelley at Boscombe, is one of the best rabbit hunters to the gun I ever shot to. Her nose is so curiously intelligent, that availing herself with the greatest quickness of the wind, she will ascertain if a considerable patch of gorse or heather contains a rabbit, and if she goes not in to put the rabbit out, you may rely upon it that there is not one there."

Mrs Scarlett was very artistic and obviously had a great sense of humour. In 1867 she drew several amusing sketches of the Italians dressed in human clothing, depicting the courtship and marriage of Vispo and Linda, two of their IGs.

The Marchioness of Waterford kept a diary and it contains at least three references to her dogs, which is why we know that her husband was not so interested in the breed as she was. Her daughter remembered some of the dogs when she was a small child in about l904 and kindly quoted from her mother's diary: (the 'T' referred to was her mother's husband):

"Dec l900 We had rather fun teaching my Italian Greyhounds to course rabbits. 'T' hated them because they always shivered and one of them 'Dante' familiarly called 'The Poet' or 'Danny' always yelled when 'T' looked at him. Stella however was much more courageous and much less shivery than the Poet, it was a real pleasure to see her gallop. 'T' often had a few rabbits caught up and then let loose to give the dogs a course. Stella took to it very kindly and killed the rabbits in fine greyhound style.

"June 1901 I exhibited my Italian Greyhounds at the Richmond Dog Show this summer and 'T' drove me down there; he was quite interested in the competition, though he had the greatest contempt for the Italians.

"Dec 1903 One of our amusements this winter was coursing rabbits with my Italian Greyhound puppies and their mother. She, Stella, was quite an expert at the game. The pups who were entered at 8 months were pretty good and it was very pretty to see them move but this did not improve and they soon grew tired of the sport........"

References to the dogs cease approximately in the winter of 1905-6, when the couple spent some time in Africa hunting wild game on safari.

In France, the poet Alphonse de Lamartine (1790-1869), born in Macon, was known to have kept Italian Greyhounds since his childhood. He spent this period in his life in the family home in Milly, as the son of a country gentleman. After schooling he lived at the manor house of Saint-Point. He then travelled in Italy, married an English lady, and then filled various diplomatic posts at Naples and Florence, becoming Foreign Minister and a leader of the Republican government. In later life he was burdened by financial worries, but in the more carefree periods of his life he was known to present his closest friends with Italian Greyhounds as gifts as a token of his friendship. It seems that many verses were written by him concerning the little dogs:

"Oh come each friend to cheer my steps
Do not be afraid that before God I will blush for you,
Lick my wet eyes, put your heart near mine
And alone to love each other, let us love little dog."

He recalled the days of his childhood in the following verse:

"I remember having in my childhood a dog for a friend,
A white levrette, with a gazelle's nose,
A coat like silk, a dove's neck,
Deep gentle eye like a human's look,
She never ate but from my hand,
Answered only to my voice, followed my steps,
Slept only on my bed, and sniffed at my place;
When I went out alone and she was left,
Cried all the time I was out
To see me longer, going or coming,
She jumped with one bound onto my windowsill,
And with both feet braced against the cold glass,
Looked all day through the frames,

'The Great Picture'. Reproduced by kind permission of Abbot Hall Art Gallery, Kendal, Cumbria, UK.

Or running round my room, she looked
For a trace, the shadow of the master she adored
The last garment I wore
My pen, my coat, my still open book,
And with ear pricked to hear better
Lay down beside it, to pass the time to my return."

Those visiting the North of England may be interested in The Great Picture of the Clifford family, (which features a small, white Italian Greyhound), now belonging to the Abbot Hall Art Gallery. This, together with more than fifty other portraits of the Clifford family and their descendants, the Tuftons, Earls of Thanet, was purchased by the Gallery from The Dowager Lady Hothfield just prior to her death. It can be seen at the Great Hall at Appleby Castle (daily from Easter until the end of September, and by appointment throughout the rest of the year).

It seems that Lady Ann Clifford commissioned the painting in 1646 when she came into her inheritance. The Tullie House Museum in Carlisle, also houses a painting of former owners of the residence when in private hands, a Mr and Mrs Dixon. The lady stands at the side of her husband, who is seated at his desk, and a little Italian Greyhound is in the chair at her side. Also in this museum is a bronze statuette, found south of Hadrian's Wall at Kirkby Thore.

Several dog skeletons have been found on Hadrian's Wall, but the archaeological authorities of the area are reluctant to confirm that they were definitely those of Italian Greyhounds. These are usually just recorded as 'large', 'medium' or 'small'. Very little work has apparently been done

*Silverplate,
(middle figure
after Mene style).*

*Florentine
marble model,
approx. twelve
inches in height.*

*Staffordshire figures (small
dog in centre possibly
Rockingham).*

*Bronze by Pierre Jukes
Mene (1810-1877).*

*Dog whip, approx
1900 (wooden handle,
silver band,
Greyhound head).*

*Left: Fawn on green base, cold cast
marble, by Earl Sherwan, USA.
Middle: Lady and dog, made in
Czechoslovakia. Right: Sitting fawn
dog, Rosenthaal, Germany.*

*Victorian silver
candle holders.*

on identification of animal bone assemblages, but several owners in the 1950s were convinced that these were IGs. Some bones of dogs have also been found in certain wells containing deposits of an apparent votive nature, and this may also reflect inherent connections between dogs and healing cults associated with wells and rivers. Bronze stauettes of IGs in a typical sitting pose have been found at Lydney Park, Gloucestershire.

Owners of the breed interested in attempting to have a collection of memorabilia are always attracted to the porcelain and bronze figures. Pierre Jules Mene (1810-1877) produced several bronzes of Italian Greyhounds in typical pose of one leg held high and head turned. All of these should have the sculptor's signature on the base to be true editions; however, there are many copies after the same style. I was very fortunate to obtain a lifesize Florentine marble model of an Italian Greyhound some years ago, purchased from a retired judge of dogs, who had originally bought it in Italy. Apparently this sort of memento was often produced as a memorial to a beloved pet, and sometimes placed on pillars in the large villas. The English Staffordshire pottery figures are much sought after. In the main, these depict Greyhounds, some carrying hares, some sitting; but many collectors, whether Italian Greyhound, Greyhound or Whippet fanciers, can appreciate these ornaments and delight in them. It is important to take care when purchasing models of this type to ascertain the age of the piece, as there are a number of modern pieces in the same style and obviously they are less valuable. There are also the finer Rosenthaal (German) and Minton (English) figures, which are so sensitively styled and the interpretation of the breed is beautifully projected. Needless to say these are also priced accordingly.

Whatever your interest in Italian Greyhounds, whether you show the breed, whether you own one or several, the historic background of IGs and the hunt for collectables is an on-going fascination. No street market, museum, book store, antique shop, art gallery, stately home, or department store is safe from our prying eyes, always on the lookout for something 'Italian'.

Chapter Thirteen

IN THE NURSERY

SHOULD YOU BREED AN IG LITTER?

If you decide that you would like to breed your very own litter of Italian Greyhounds, it is obviously important to assess all the pros and cons. Supposing the litter are all males when you really want a bitch? What will happen if your bitch has a big litter? Generally, Italian bitches produce anything from one to four puppies, but litters of five and even eight have been known. Will it cause problems in your household when the new puppies start to take up more space and become increasingly mischievous? Supposing no suitable homes come along, can you keep the puppies? Can you have any puppies back that may not fit in or when their new owners' circumstances change? Only you, the owner, know the answer to these all-important questions.

If you are still keen to breed a litter, it is important to read as much as possible on the whole subject of breeding before you decide to go ahead. The pedigree of both your bitch and her prospective mate should also be studied. This should have occupied your thoughts for months before the bitch is ready for mating. Remember that no dog or bitch is perfect, so in taking care to avoid a particular fault in one line, you may introduce another defect. It is certainly worth seeking the advice of experienced owners and breeders.

Never fall into the trap of believing your bitch needs a litter.

If she is perfectly happy and content and has a loving owner, she may well prove a loving and capable mother, but it is not a necessity for her good health. The same goes for a male IG. Few males would ignore the opportunity to mate a bitch, but they will not suffer if they are never allowed to do so. In fact, if you have other bitches coming in season it may be a nuisance if your dog becomes obsessed with the idea that he is going to mate them all!

It may be appropriate to mention here that if you have a young male who you intend to use at stud at some point, he should not be allowed to pester in-season bitches and then be reprimanded by his owner. If he is continually deprived of acting out his natural instinct, when the time comes that you do want him to mate either one of your own bitches or someone else's, you may find him reluctant. It is best to keep males and in-season bitches as separate as possible during the season.

A bitch is supposedly in oestrus for twenty-one days, but beware of the exceptions. I have returned bitches 'to the fold' only to find them far more attractive to the dogs at that stage than before! Always reintroduce the bitch freshly bathed, and supply clean bedding, but never leave her alone with a male until he is definitely not showing any interest.

On two occasions I have had unplanned matings when the bitches were twenty-four days from the beginning of the season. In one of these instances I had to have the bitch injected against having puppies because she was far too small. This resulted in another 'season', which ultimately altered her cycle so completely that she had to have a hysterectomy. In the second, more recent case, I left the bitch and fortunately she did not conceive. However, it is never safe to assume a bitch will not have puppies because it is so late in a season. I cannot stress sufficiently that in every generalisation made about dogs, there are always exceptions!

A novice breeder should always seek the advice of a vet to check that the bitch is of suitable size and is in good health. The bitch should be in excellent health if you are planning to breed from her – neither too fat nor too thin. Prior to her season she should have been wormed. This should be a regular part of her health care in any case, but it is most important that she is wormed at this time. If other dogs are kept they should all be wormed at the same time, and their exercise area should be kept scrupulously clean at all times. It has often been found in Italian Greyhounds that dogs of very senior years still make good stud dogs, particularly if mated to younger bitches.

The size of the litter, and the size of the individual puppies, can be difficult to determine. The biggest dogs do not necessarily produce enormous puppies, as many of us have discovered. The larger sound specimens have always been considered necessary among the stud force to ensure soundness in the breed. The bitch must be typical in every way, and so, indeed, should the intended sire of the litter.

Italian Greyhound bitches do not always have their first season at six months of age, like many larger breeds. Some have been known to be nearly two years before coming on heat for the first time. However, if you assume that the average bitch comes into season at ten months, then it is wise to wait until about the third season before you mate her. She should certainly be no younger than eighteen months of age when she has her first litter.

THE MATING

WHEN IS THE BITCH READY?
At the commencement of the heat, the vulva will begin to swell and the bitch will probably need to urinate more often. Initially there will be pink staining on the bedding, and it is useful to use white bedding at this time so that you can detect the first day of colour. All breeders will have their very own definite idea as to the best day that a bitch should be mated – and so do most of the bitches! On average the tenth to thirteenth day is most commonly allocated, although I know some breeders who are absolutely adamant that their IG bitches are ready to mate much sooner than that. In the early days of my own dog breeding I think I tended to err on the side of being too early rather than being too late.

In fact, the bitch is probably more likely not to conceive through being mated too early than too late. The vulva will swell to perhaps three times its normal size, and when she is ready for mating it tends to look slightly smaller and softer, and often the discharge is less. However, I have found that if a bitch is mated the discharge often starts to flow more freely again. As the season progresses the discharge will tend to be more brown in colour than red. The bitch should be kept away from other males after being mated. Do not think that she will assume she is 'spoken for', because that will not be the case.

She must not be allowed to be mated by another male. If this happens, a true pedigree cannot be produced and, strictly speaking, both sires should be made known to the Kennel Club. You may feel that you would like the bitch to be mated more than once. Again, all breeders have their different theories as to the wisdom of this. If it is a good mating, then one should suffice. It only takes the merest speck of sperm from the male to fertilize the eggs and produce puppies.

HANDLING THE STUD DOG

From the point of view of the owners of the stud dog, I would say, do not rush him. If the dog is inexperienced, then allow him and the bitch to get acquainted. If the bitch is a little anti-social, then it is a good idea to keep her on a lead and allow the male to sniff all the appropriate parts and hopefully arouse her interest.

If you have a good, experienced male then it does help if the dog is allowed to mount the bitch and is then lifted off again before penetration takes place. This helps the female to realise the weight of the dog, and become aware of what is going on. The vulva should be tipped outwards, using the tips of your fingers to ease the placement of the dog's penis into position. The hand should be held under the bitch's tummy, with the fingertips pointing outwards under the back legs. In the case of different heights, cushions or newspapers haphazardly stacked can make it easier for the two to get into the most comfortable position.

THE TIE

Once the dog has tied he cannot pull away while the bitch's muscles hold him, and if the bitch starts to struggle she must be held steady, keeping your hands firmly on her shoulders to keep her front feet down, thus preventing her from pulling away from the dog and hurting him. Many males like to 'turn'. This means that they drop their front feet over the side of the bitch and turn themselves around, still held by the bitch, but the two dogs finish up with their rears end to end. This is quite normal, but with a new stud dog, do be careful that he does not try to do this before he is sufficiently tied with the bitch. In some cases it may be better to keep him held just across the bitch's back with his front feet on the floor at her side rather than allowing a complete turn.

We have found some bitches' owners, particularly those who are new to the business, make rather too much fuss of their bitches, talking and fussing them too much, and this only causes a distraction. Let the two keep their sole interest on each other and not on the humans present. If an owner accompanying a novice bitch is disturbing her too much, it may be better if the stud dog owner is left to manage the mating without extra assistance – of course, the bitch's owner should be invited to see the pair when a tie has taken place.

A stud dog that is mistreated will be very wary of mating another bitch, so if a bitch is rather fractious it can help if an old sock or stocking is placed over her head during the mating. This will allow her to breath, but the fact that she cannot see often has a soothing effect. It also prevents her from biting the dog or anyone else, which she may be tempted to do. I recall a Champion bitch that was conceived in my own home using this method. Some bitches will stand as still as a rock, and they are worth their weight in gold. If an inexperienced male is allowed to become over-excited, it is best to put him to bed for fifteen minutes or so to calm him down, and then recommence the proceedings. I have found that this also works if a dog is reluctant; this break sometimes helps to gee him up.

AFTER THE MATING

After the mating has taken place and the dog has pulled away voluntarily, it is a good idea for his owner to gently wash him underneath, to remove all smells of the bitch, especially when other males are kept on the premises, but this attention to hygiene should be observed in all situations. A small titbit can be given as a reward, and then the dog should be taken away and put to rest, out of sight of the bitch. Some owners like to pick the bitch up and tip her on her back. There is a theory that this enables the sperm to linger; whether true or false, it does no harm. The bitch should then be allowed to return to her bed to clean herself, and left confined for a couple of hours. She should not be allowed to urinate during this time.

THE PREGNANCY

Now both owners have to await results. Sixty-three days, the average duration of the pregnancy seems a long time when you are waiting – but try to relax and hope for the best. For the first four weeks or so there is no need to change the bitch's diet. As time progresses, the quantity should be increased and vitamins and any other supplements can be added, as prescribed by your vet.

Italian Greyhounds can easily disguise one or two puppies in the womb until the last few days. However, I tend to feel that if you are really in doubt by seven weeks, then the bitch is probably not in whelp. A singleton can confuse the issue. I had a small bitch, who produced one normal puppy, but to outsiders she looked no different from normal during her pregnancy. The best indication can be gained by weighing the bitch. Each full grown puppy weighs between five to nine ounces, and placentas weigh about the same. Later in the pregnancy, at about six to seven weeks, depending upon the size of the litter, small movements may be seen which will get more and more vigorous as the pregnancy progresses.

It is quite common for bitches to suffer from morning sickness, in the same way as some pregnant women. It does not do any harm, although you do feel very sorry for them. The bitch may vomit a small amount of yellow or white substance at about three weeks of pregnancy, and it is quite likely that she will decline to eat. This latter problem is really hard to cope with. I am assured by vets that the bitch will not starve and neither will the puppies, but it always grieves me to see an Italian refuse food when she is having to cope with the ever-increasing demands on her bodies by her puppies. If you are not happy with the bitch then you must seek advice, and sometimes the vet will give an injection of vitamins which may boost the appetite.

One of my bitches refused proper meals from the third to the sixth week of her pregnancy but when she started to eat again she soon made up for lost time! As IGs generally prefer two smaller meals to one large meal, the feeding regime for the pregnant bitch can remain the same for the first three weeks. Between three and five weeks this can be increased by about a third, providing the bitch is willing to eat, and not setting about a hunger strike, as some do at this stage. At about this time one of the proprietary milk substitutes can be given, or goat's milk (supplied dried or frozen in many areas, if fresh is not available).

At five to six weeks the bitch may appreciate a smaller, third meal being introduced, and this pattern should be continued to the end of her pregnancy. While she is devouring all that is being offered and her motions are firm, it is safe to assume that you are feeding the correct amount. If diarrhoea develops it is likely that either the milk substitute is not suitable to the bitch's

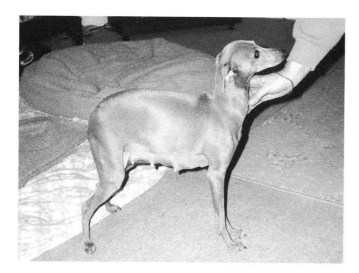

Ch. Cenere la Traviata of Caccia, Owned by Mrs L. Loh and bred by Mrs J. Harper. Best of Breed Crufts 1990, pictured sixty-two days into her pregnancy.

metabolism, or the quantity of food is excessive. Adjustments should therefore be made accordingly.

When the due date approaches, it pays to be ready about a week before whelping is expected. This probably means the bitch will keep you waiting, but it is essential to have a sterile bed prepared, and all the necessary equipment that will be so essential when the time comes. As the pregnancy progresses a clear, sticky discharge is often seen. Do not worry if you miss it because some bitches are so fastidious that they clean themselves before you notice it. However, if you watch your bitch when she has urinated in the garden the discharge will often appear hanging from the vulva. If this should change in appearance, to red or brown or green, then inform your vet immediately. This could indicate a problem and speedy attention may be necessary.

THE WHELPING

In general, you should try not to be too anxious when the bitch begins the first stage of whelping. Initially you may not even be aware that she has begun. A lot of books on the subject say that the bitch will refuse to eat, but certainly over the years my dogs have disproved this theory. The bitch may actually appear to be rather quiet and different in character for about three days and you will be on tenterhooks the whole time, even staying up all night, only to find that she will go to full term and whelp during the day. That is the fun of having puppies – and you can always laugh about it afterwards!

When you are choosing a suitable place for your bitch to whelp, you must decide on whatever arrangement suits you and the bitch best. If the whelping can be conducted in the peace of your own home, it is far better for the all-round comfort of the bitch. If you have more than one IG or any other pets, you may find you will have to exclude them from a particular area and encourage the bitch to rest there. This will hopefully persuade her that this is the place to have her puppies.

Other pets must be excluded when whelping commences; under normal circumstances they are probably the best of companions but this is a very private time for the bitch, and any intrusion may cause an extra complication. Some bitches can be very possessive at the beginning, and it is better to foresee this rather than risk upset at a crucial moment. Too much bustling activity from other members of the household can also be disturbing for the bitch, so either make arrangements for others to keep relatively inconspicuous, or arrange for the whelping to take place in another room.

The bitch must be allowed to concentrate on the proceedings. Try and carry on as normal, even if you think she may be 'doing something'; sitting and staring at her will not help either of you. For this reason I like my bitches to whelp in an area where I will be occupied, but I can keep them under observation. It seems to me that bitches can almost halt proceedings if they decide to, because something attracts their attention. This theory is impossible to prove, but certainly nature cannot be rushed and the bitch will not have her litter until she feels ready.

When you first notice the bitch's back shimmering – by which I mean a tremor like a shiver running down her back, even though she may be tucked up, then it is likely that the first stage of labour is underway. The tremors will eventually turn into obvious strains when she is bearing down, and these should be timed. The more regular and faster they are, the more imminent the first arrival. She will probably do a lot of nesting, i.e. tearing up the bedding with her mouth and claws, and therefore it is essential to have soft material so that she does not damage herself.

I prepare a warm, clean box with bedding ready for the puppies when they are born, and I have a separate box with pieces of sheeting and paper for the bitch to tear. A cardboard box with the front cut out will suffice, and this can be replaced if necessary. This 'nesting' does seem to satisfy a natural instinct, and it is important for the bitch to be allowed to be able to do it. She may have a mad tearing fit, and then almost cover herself up with the remains and sleep again for a bit. This could continue for a couple of hours. There are many books on the market which show in great detail the procedures of whelping, and I do advise new breeders to read as much as possible before the event and, better still, ask a more experienced breeder to join you for the whelping. This should be someone the bitch has met before, rather than introducing a stranger at this sensitive time.

After regular and concentrated straining, a rather jelly-like bag will appear. Novice breeders may think the bitch is straining to open her bowels because this is how it looks. I think that some bitches get confused in the early contraction period, and may repeatedly ask to go out as they do not wish to soil their beds. This water bag lubricates the canal and is the barrier of protection between the puppies inside the mother and the outside world. The bag will appear and disappear for some time, and if it can be left unbroken for a good while this is helpful, but often it is broken by the bitch while she is fidgeting about, and you will soon see her licking furiously and the bedding will be wet. It is helpful to have a number of pieces of paper towel and pieces of towel or sheeting so that the bitch can be kept as comfortable and dry as possible. The breeder can replace the damp pieces during the whelping.

Sometimes it can take two to three hours of furious straining before a puppy emerges. It will either be feet first, which is known as a breech birth, or head first. Occasionally there is only one foot, or some other more difficult presentation, but as there are so many different things that can happen at this stage, only experience will tell you how the birth is progressing. It is very useful to have a piece of towel, absolutely clean, to grasp whatever is available of the puppy. This gives a good purchase on the pup, and if the owner can keep a grip on it, will prevent the puppy slipping back inside the bitch, if there is some difficulty on her part in pushing it out. If the puppy is head first and this can be seen through the covering sac, or if the sac has burst and the head is visible, it usually comes forth with only a little assistance. Most bitches can manage

The whelping: the first puppy about to be born. The sac should be removed immediately if the bitch is reluctant. Dark green and brown staining from the placenta fluids is normal.

alone but many do not object to their owner helping to remove the puppy. Never pull too hard; give each contraction time to do its work in pushing the puppy further down the canal and into the opening. It is essential to have well-scrubbed hands when handling the dam and the pups.

If a foot or a pair of feet appear first, then it is even more essential to hang on, as sometimes the puppy will appear to be entering the world and then the feet disappear up inside again, and the whole process will take much longer. Assistance in keeping the presentation moving will be most beneficial, and towelling will give a firm grip without hurting the whelp. Newborn puppies can stand a fair amount of pulling, but be careful not to squeeze the feet or other parts, as I have known a puppy's foot to be damaged in this way. The puppy should always be pulled outwards and round towards the mother's stomach, never try to pull it straight out. Sometimes if two puppies are coming quickly together, it can be very hectic, particularly for a novice breeder, and that is why I feel – for the benefit of both the owner and the bitch – the support of an experienced friend is worth its weight in gold at this time. Books are very useful, but it is not the same as having a friend there to actually *show* you what to do.

The placenta should be attached to the puppy, and this will appear as a dark-red, black mass, fixed to the pup by the umbilical cord. It is essential to make sure each puppy has a placenta as well. A retained placenta can cause severe illness in the bitch. Sometimes bitches will eat them so quickly, it is difficult to keep track. In my opinion, it is not wise to allow the bitch to eat all the placentas. I usually remove them as quickly as possible, as I find some bitches can get a bit 'wild' in their actions if they start gobbling up the placentas, even though I know some breeders believe they contain essential natural elements. The bitch will often bite through the umbilical cord, and care must be taken with a maiden bitch to ensure that in her excitement, she does not bite it too close to the belly of the puppy. If you can intervene, the cord should be held tight, about two inches or so from the puppy in order to cut off the blood supply. Either cut or tear the coird, and tie off with cotton.

When the puppy emerges, it must be roughly dried with the towelling to make it cry – rather like a human baby. This yell will help clear its mouth and lungs of any mucus. Tip the pup upside down and rub it in your hands in the towel. If there has been any difficulty in the birth, which does not happen often in Italians, and the puppy seems lifeless, all these procedures can make the difference between life and death. A lifeless-looking puppy can suddenly yell, and surprise you. Breech births are very common in dogs, tail or feet first, as already stated.

On the rare occasions when a puppy cannot be passed by the bitch then a vet must be consulted, as a caesarian section may be necessary. Fortunately, this is not a common occurrence with IGs, but if the need arises you can ask your vet if you can be on hand in order that you may assist with the resuscitation of the puppies. The vet's main concern will be with the welfare of the dam, but it is most essential that the newborn puppies are roughly dried, encouraged to cry to clear their lungs and kept warm.

In a normal delivery the intervals between puppies being born can be an hour or two or a matter of minutes, but never let the bitch strain hard for more than two to three hours without seeking advice. Sometimes the owner believes the bitch is in distress when it is only nature taking its course. However, the bitch could be in genuine distress, so it is better to be safe than sorry and to get expert advice. Sometimes a pituitary injection may be given to speed up the contractions, but a vet will not do this if there is a reason for the delay, such as a wrongly presented puppy or an obstruction of some sort.

When a bitch has delivered her first pup and is busy straining with more contractions, she may show no interest in the new arrival. Some newborn puppies make a lot of noise, and this can distress the bitch, particularly if she cannot see them. I always place the puppy near to her on a dry bed so that she knows it is safe, and then put it out of the way if she starts nesting again, as some bitches do between births. Many bitches stand up and drop the puppy as it is being born, others will lie on their side in the box to produce the puppy. Each bitch acts slightly differently and each whelping is also slightly different. The puppies will aim for the teats of the bitch which contain the valuable colostrum, which is so important for them, as it passes on the bitch's immunities. In between births and contractions, allow the puppies to suckle at will, as this will help the mother to contract .

Italian Greyhound puppies are amazingly strong and almost seem to walk around the box when they are newborn. You would be forgiven for thinking they were Labradors, for they do not resemble their adult shape at all. I have bred a number of other toy breed puppies, and they were all very backward compared with Italians. Newborn IG puppies weigh in the region of five to nine ounces, but sometimes more or sometimes less. To tell the truth, I have found that this newborn weight has little bearing on the eventual size and weight of the adult dog. However, many of us keep a note of puppy weights in order to compare from litter to litter, as sometimes in families of dogs it is possible to obtain a guide to eventual size. This is a difficult area in IGs and size is one of the hardest factors to estimate when purchasing a young puppy.

Size considerations apart, it is a good idea to keep a notebook handy during the whelping in the event of any problems arising. A vet will need a precise record of events in order to take the appropriate action. Each newborn puppy should be examined for cleft palate, dew claws, and kinks in their tails. It should be checked all over to make sure it is whole in every way, and to find out its sex. If the puppy has a defect, it is far kinder to put it to sleep when it is newborn, rather than having to make the decision when it is older.

The process of whelping will take some hours and can never be rushed. Some bitches take longer than others, and some bitches are capable of hiding all the early stages, and before the breeder knows she is in labour, she produces a pup! One of our bitches did just this. 'Rosie' was sleeping beside my bed, as do all my bitches if they are due to whelp. A couple of days prior to her due date, she jumped on the bed at 4am and by 4.20 we had two puppies! This is the exception rather than the rule, I might add. When Rosie's daughter had her two litters she kept me hanging around for days before the due date, looking thoroughly miserable, and giving the impression she might be 'doing something'. Even experienced owners can never be absolutely sure when things are going to 'start'.

My very first Italian kept me up for a couple of nights because I was so certain she was about to start. I eventually retired to bed, with her sleeping next to me, when she suddenly awoke me by jumping up on the bed, with the biggest 'grin' on her face. At least she had the kindness to tell me she was ready to produce now!

THE FIRST DAYS

When the whelping is finally over and you are sure there are no more puppies on the way, allow the bitch outside to urinate, and quickly transfer the puppies to their ready-prepared clean, warm bed. When the mother dashes back in, which I know she will, settle her down and then offer her a drink of whatever milky preparation you have decided to use, and leave her in peace with her new family. Some bitches do not take to motherhood immediately; they fidget and whine and keep turning the bedding around, and you find one puppy attached to a teat and the other under the bed. This is quite normal, particularly in maiden bitches, and some do make better mothers than others. I also think the bitch may be in some discomfort until her milk is flowing properly, which is not until the third day.

If the bitch is not settling with her puppies, do not allow her to keep leaving them to get on your knee. Rearrange the bed, place the puppies conveniently close to the mother and leave them secluded. An enclosed cage with a roof is the most convenient housing after whelping, and sometimes it helps if you drape a curtain around the sides so that the bitch cannot be distracted.

All newborn puppies have their ears sticking out.

You will often find that when the bitch is left to her own devices she will sort herself out, even if you have to go through the whole performance every time she is allowed out. It is better to use one rigid type of bedding rather than having several loose pieces, which could suffocate a puppy, particularly with these fidgety females. If you are using the fleecy hessian-backed type of bedding, it may be necessary to fasten it to the base of the bed with sticky-sided tape. I have found that if you have a television or radio on near the family, the noise can soothe the bitch, without distracting her from her task. However, most Italian Greyhounds are super mothers and,

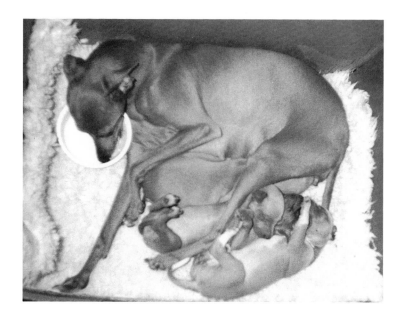

*The litter
at three
weeks.*

in fact, there have been several instances of them fostering offspring from others dogs.

When the bitch is out of the way doing her own toilet, do make sure she is cleaning the puppies properly; it is essential that the anus is kept clean. I have known some bitches that find this distasteful in the beginning of their motherhood, and a puppy can become very uncomfortable. If this happens, then clean the excreta away from under the pup's tale with cotton wool (cotton) and oil, or margarine, or something similar (it is important not to wet the puppy too much) and usually the taste of the oil will encourage the mother to do the job properly.

Again, any early reluctance in this department is usually soon overcome. Check to ensure that the milk supply is flowing. If there is only one puppy the surplus teats can become hard and engorged if they are not regularly milked by the owner. A gentle squeezing of the teats that do not appear to be in use can prevent mastitis from setting in. After a few days the supply evens out to suit the requirements of the offspring.

Eclampsia affects bitches of all breeds from time to time, and although I have not had first-hand experience of this, others in the breed have been severely troubled by the problem. The condition is caused by a calcium deficiency, and the dam is unable to store sufficient calcium in her body to supply the needs of herself and her pups.

This usually occurs three to six weeks after whelping, and the bitch appears very restless, sometimes even screaming out. The eyes may appear bloodshot, and paralysis of the legs and excessive panting may occur. This panting is not to be confused with the panting that can be observed in some bitches in the first twenty-four hours after whelping, which, I think, is often caused by sheer excitement and tiredness. If eclampsia is suspected, a vet must be contacted immediately as the condition can prove fatal. The vet's instructions must be followed implicitly, which may involve separating the bitch from her puppies. Usually the treatment will involve administering large doses of calcium.

Assuming all is well, the new family must be placed somewhere warm, quiet and comfortable. Do not roast them, as this is just as uncomfortable as being too cold. Overhead lamps can be used, or heated dog beds are available; all breeders have their own ideas. The temperature must also be comfortable for the bitch; if she is too warm she will move away from the puppies, and this is not desirable. It is also important to remember that too much artificial heat on her skin and coat will dry the skin and she will lose her coat. If you can keep her warm enough, without too much added heat, this is beneficial. This should not be difficult in homes that have central heating.

Good food is essential for the bitch, who will in turn supply her puppies. All this will have been organised in advance. Remember that any 'treat' given to the mother will go straight through to her milk, so do not be surprised to find that the puppies cry and appear to have loose motions if you suddenly change the bitch's diet.

Dew claws on the puppies need to be removed at about three to five days. They are usually to be found on the front legs only, but do check the back ones as a precaution. The puppies' toe nails will grow very quickly and they must be kept cut so as not to scratch the dam. You will see how the puppies knead the bitch when they are suckling, and this can be quite painful if the nails are not kept short. Regular weighing is useful to check the growth of the puppies. Puppies, like human babies, lose weight initially, but by the end of the first week a puppy will usually have doubled its birth weight.

REARING THE LITTER

While nursing her puppies, the dam may be reluctant to leave them to eat during the first two or three days, and she may expect her adoring owner to hold the dish out to her inside the bed so that she does not have to leave the litter. Listen to the voice of experience! The meals should be very similar in quantity to those she has been eating at the end of her pregnancy, with plenty of milky drinks, using the same brand of milk powder as has been used during the pregnancy. Fresh water should always be available within the whelping quarters.

Some bitches will regurgitate food for their offspring. Do not be alarmed; this is just nature's way of introducing puppies to the weaning process. As the puppies grow and become more demanding, the bitch's meals should be increased in quantity; she will most probably need two or three times her usual rations. Again, the dam's excreta will indicate if the quantity is about right.

Weaning should begin at two to three weeks. This depends on how many puppies there are in the litter, and how good a mother the bitch is. Start with finely chopped or minced beef, offered from your fingers; just give a mere taste initially. The puppy may spit it out, or it may try to take your finger too! Italians are not usually difficult to wean, but do not try and rush it. Gradually introduce a taste of solid food once a day for two or three days, graduating to a teaspoonful or so during the third week, probably twice a day. I believe it is best to stick to the meaty side of things to begin with, rather than introducing artificial milk too soon, as nothing can better the milk the dam is providing, while she still has it.

When the puppies are about three weeks of age a worming syrup can be given. Roundworms are present in most puppies and nursing bitches, whether visible or not. These are anything from three to six inches long, pointed at both ends, and creamy-white in colour. Hormones released during pregnancy encourage their activity and some will transfer to the puppies; more larvae will come via the bitch's milk; she will lick her puppies clean, and, in turn, remove the excreta from her brood, and so the cycle perpetuates itself. At five weeks, providing the puppies are fit and strong and growing well, a worming programme should be commenced. The dam should also be given the medication. These days it is not necessary to starve dogs, as it was at one time, but occasionally some pups do regurgitate tablets if they are not sufficiently crushed. If the food containing the crushed tablet is retained for ten minutes or so, it should have served its purpose. The dosage should be accurate, and this is defined by the weight of the puppy; your vet will advise. Remember the puppy is growing all the time, and therefore the dosage must be amended accordingly. The worming programme should be carried out again at about four to six months of age and thereafter about once every nine months, unless obvious signs of infestation are apparent.

Tape worms are less common in puppies that are kept in clean domestic circumstances, but feeding raw offal should be avoided. Heavily infected puppies may regurgitate worms as well as defecate them. After worming, the puppies should be closely observed and the offending material disposed of immediately. Do not allow other dogs to sniff or otherwise come in contact with the excreta.

When the puppies are about four to five weeks old they should be accepting perhaps five small 'meals', a couple of which can be made up of baby cereal and the proprietary milk the dam has been given in pregnancy. The amounts will naturally vary according to the size of the puppies, but a desertspoonful per puppy, per meal, is a reasonable guide. If the puppies devour all you give them and have firm motions, then try a little more, but in small stages. By now the dam should be given a little less food each week.

Her milk supply will be determined by the demand of the little ones, and the amount of food consumed by her. As the pups eat more of the food offered by the breeder, her milk drinks should also be reduced. In this way the puppies will wean naturally, and the dam's milk supply will gradually cease. The puppies will be eating more and having the same brand of milk as a drink, and the bitch will be able to spend less time with them.

There are so many good brands of dog food available with added vitamins, including the varied 'complete diets' that it is impossible to recommend a particular diet. The main criterion must be to always buy the best. However, if the owner decides to use fresh meat and wholemeal biscuit, this should not mean best steak. Puppies need some of the fat that is found on the cheaper cuts of beef or lamb, and although they will love chicken, for instance, it is a good idea to feed red meat as well. Another point to bear in mind if you are feeding fresh meat is that it may prove a nuisance when you are travelling, if the puppies are not used to the 'convenience' foods specially manufactured for dogs. Always try and keep the puppies roly-poly fat if you can, although as their legs grow they will appear less well covered at some stages.

When the litter is seven weeks old, the dam may only be sleeping with them. As the puppies' teeth become sharper, she will feel them while they suckle, and she will find them less endearing, and she may not always be in the mood for the rough and tumble of her increasingly active brood. From four to five weeks onwards, she should be allowed to have a short period away from the puppies after they have fed and cleaned them, if she so wishes. This is where a large cage with a roof is useful as it prevents the risk of the pups jumping out. It also provides a place where they can play out of harm's way, and a place to rest, which is equally important.

If the owner is anxious for the bitch to return to the show ring, the easier you can make this transition period, the more likely she is to return to a good shape, without any harm being done to the litter. However, it is important to be patient, and it is better to have a few extra weeks out of the ring, and a happy, contented mother and family. The puppies and their dam should be allowed to take as long or as short a time as they need for this changeover. Breeders should always be aware of the possible dangers of infection that could result in allowing a bitch to return to the ring, and then mixing with young, uninoculated puppies. A puppy's natural immunity from infection gained from the dam ceases at about eight weeks.

At eight weeks of age, four meals should be sufficient for the puppies. This regime should be continued, with the amounts being increased as they grow, using the criteria of formed motions, nice, glossy skin and plump bodies, and bright eyes to tell you that you are feeding the correct rations. By the time a puppy is about four months old, it will usually start to leave one of its meals of its own accord, usually it is one of the cereal meals that goes first. Basically, it is important to bear in mind that a growing puppy will be eating two or three times the amount of an adult dog. Owners who do not appreciate this can severely restrict the growth of their puppies, and growth cannot be put on later. The essentials must be given from the pregnancy through to the birth, and throughout the puppy's growth period.

By six months the pup will usually be down to two meals, with perhaps a milky drink as well. Most puppies will continue to drink milk for longer if it is offered without the cereal. Needless to say, a puppy will sometimes take a dislike to something it has eaten perfectly well previously, and because you want to keep your puppy well covered, you may find yourself chopping and changing the diet to suit its whims, particularly if you wish to show your puppy. The trouble is that this sometimes causes a puppy to become even more faddy.

In this situation, try not to offer titbits, and if you can harden your heart and pick up dishes with left food, this often makes a puppy realise that it is now or never! Competition for food is often a good way to keep weight on IG pups; two pups will often eat better than one on its own. Lightly scrambled eggs, grated cheese, and boiled rice are all acceptable additions to the diet of puppies and growing dogs. Be careful with eggs, however, as occasionally a puppy fails to digest them, and in such instances they should not be offered. A little honey, stirred into the milky foods, is also a good nutritional contribution to the diet.

As the puppies grow they should get used to lots of handling, and talking to them will encourage the bond between dog and human. Never let the mother feel left out of the proceedings; she must still be your star, as without her there would not be any puppies. Table training should also begin at an early age. In a nutshell, breeding is all about providing good food for the dam and her family, and all the care and attention you can give. Puppies are great time-wasters, and you will spend hour after hour just watching your litter of Italians – you will delight in their every movement and all other household tasks will become secondary!

Chapter Fourteen

HEALTH AND GENERAL WELFARE

In the main, Italian Greyhounds do not suffer from many ailments that beset other members of the canine family; however, to assist the first-time owner I have drawn attention to some of the more common conditions. Obviously, every owner will consult their own veterinary surgeon, and methods do vary. For instance, the use of homoeopathic remedies is becoming more widespread. But whichever path is chosen, the care of the little Italian Greyhound is always paramount. It is useful to have a medical book on canine diseases, which may be used as a source of reference in order to prevent undue worry, but in the main it is wise to seek expert advice if a problem crops up.

Once you have found a vet with whom you have a good rapport, he (or she) will become a very important person in the life of your Italian Greyhound. Obviously you hope that you will not need to visit the surgery too often, but when help is needed it is important that you have total confidence in your vet. The caring owner should be able to inform the vet of the precise facts concerning a dog's condition, and daily observation should mean that any changes in general health and welfare are noted immediately. This means that any treatment that is required will be fast and effective. It is sensible to ask politely if your IG can be examined in your arms, whenever this is practical. A dog standing on a table may otherwise associate any unpleasant injections etc., with being handled by a judge. Most vets are quite happy to go along with this request.

Many of the routine tasks at home that require holding your IG for treatment may be easier to perform if you wrap the dog in a towel, crossed over under the chin, quite tightly, and the ends wrapped around the dog to keep its long legs out of the way. It can seem as if a dog has twenty sets of legs if it is allowed to struggle, but if it is hemmed in, this often makes the dog calmer and more controlled, and the treatment can therefore be carried out much faster.

ANAL GLAND INFLAMMATION
This can cause distress if it is not attended to. Dogs suffering from this condition often drag their rear ends along the ground, or an abscess appears just below and to the side of the tail. An abscess of this type can be treated at home by bathing the area with cotton wool (cotton) dipped

in warm, salt water. Slight pressure should be applied to the side of the affected area, and the abscess will burst and the offending matter be released. Continue with this procedure for two or three days, keeping the hole open until the area is clean. Attention to the dog's diet may be necessary in order to make sure sufficient roughage is included. These glands should then empty themselves naturally.

ARTHRITIS

This is common in older dogs when a stiffening of the joints becomes apparent. It is essential to prevent the IG from lying in draughts or on damp flooring. After bathing always make sure the dog is thoroughly dry.

BALDNESS

This can be a problem with some Italians; it sometimes occurs in old age, but it can also affect younger dogs. Unfortunately, so far, nobody has found a total cure for it. It seems that the darker red fawn and the white coats are less prone to the problem, and it also appears to be more prevalent when there is a lack of sunshine. The IG certainly thrives in a warm and sunny atmosphere. I have found that rubbing coconut oil or mink oil into the coat is the best solution. Some owners have tried baby oil on the body coat, or on the tips of ears if they have become bald because a fellow IG has been sucking them, but this is not a good idea. The baby oil does not suit the skin and many have found that the skin seems dryer after use. Either one of the oils already mentioned should be used, or the thicker face creams available. The baldness seems to run down the back and over the flanks, and I am sure the IG's habit of covering itself up does not help this problem.

CRYPTORCHIDISM

A male dog should have two normal testicles descended in the scrotum. Occasionally only one appears or neither. When purchasing a puppy of eight to ten weeks, the testicles should be visible, even if not actually in the scrotum. It is not advisable to use a cryptorchid or monorchid at stud, as it is felt the condition could be hereditary. It is only in later life that it may bother the dog, and growths may form. When you are first ring-training a puppy you may find that when the practice judge handles the pup's rear end to check that it is entire, the dog will retract the testicles. Provided this is only a temporary phase, it does not matter. It has been known for puppies to fail to become fully 'entire' until nearly a year old, but this is the exception. My own experience has been that if there is still doubt at nine months, it is unlikely that the fault will correct.

EARS

These should be regularly examined for any signs of mites. Discharge of any sort should be removed with cotton wool (cotton) buds and warm water, and advice should be taken from medical experts if there is any unpleasant smell. Ear-drops may be necessary.

EPILEPSY OR FAINTING FITS

There is a difference between these two conditions, and Italian Greyhounds, like many other breeds, can have either. It is certainly beyond dispute that there are cases of epilepsy in nearly all breeds. A dog suffering from epilepsy may start to stagger and then its limbs become rigid; it may have a series of fits, shaking all over. Its claws will clamp, and it may pass urine or faeces. The jaws are often tightly clamped together, and there is frothing at the mouth. These fits may start at a young age, or not occur until later years. In cases of fainting, caused by heart disease or because of stress caused to the heart through major surgery, the dog may act in a similar manner, but it will probably not froth at the mouth, or lose control of its bowel and urinary tract. Stressful situations can bring on an attack.

It is best to take advice of your vet as to methods of treatment. Many owners have had dogs for many years who suffer from such an affliction, and they are quite able to cope. When the dog has recovered from the fit, it seems none the worse. It is only if the quality of the dog's life is impaired that it may be necessary for it to be put to sleep. Incidentally, do not be misled by the jerking and twitching that occurs when a dog is asleep – little puppies often jerk quite grotesquely in their sleep – but these are quite natural actions of all dogs. If your dog should have an epileptic fit, never try and put your fingers in its mouth to unclamp its jaws, as you may receive an unintentional bite. Just tilt the head to one side so that it does not choke, and hold the dog in a towel or a blanket to reassure it, until it is recovered. Medication in severe cases can help.

EYES

These should always be bright and clear. If you notice the 'whites' of the eyes appearing bloodshot or yellow in colour then advice should be sought. Progressive Retinal Atrophy (known as PRA or Night Blindness) has been found in the breed by an American breeder, who chose very valiantly to publicise the condition. A number of breeds do suffer from this hereditary disease, and many owners are now having their dogs checked and certified free, before breeding from them. None of the IGs tested in the UK have been found with the disease, but we should always admire owners who are brave enough to share their knowledge of unpleasant facts, as well as accepting the glories in the ring, as this is the only way in which breeds will be kept as healthy as man can achieve.

FALSE/PHANTOM PREGNANCY

Occasionally, whether a bitch has been mated or not, approximately nine weeks after the end of her season she may appear to have milk in her teats, she may have increased in weight, she may appear lethargic, or sick, and in extreme cases she may be possessive about her toys and sleeping box. On no account should the teats be squeezed to remove the fluid, as this will merely serve to stimulate. Various tricks can be tried to dissuade these 'would-be mums' from their maternal thoughts. Increased amounts of exercise and interesting outings at impromptu moments can help. Try to keep the bitch occupied as much as possible, for this is as much a mental state as a physical one. Her food intake should be reduced, and do not offer extra drinks of milk or tea. Discourage her from moping about as much as possible.

There are some homoeopathic remedies which have proved very useful at this time, and these seem to suit some females. Occasionally a vet may prescribe some various mineral salts to add to the bitch's food, which can be helpful. Injections of hormones are not to be recommended, unless they are a last resort. Unnatural interference can upset the bitch's hormone cycle, and if you intend to breed from her at a later date this could cause difficulties in getting her pregnant. If the bitch is not intended for breeding, I suggest that when she is in peak condition, midway between her second and third season or third and fourth season, it may be better to spay her.

If pregnancy is the ultimate aim, then the owner may just have to put up with the rather unsightly figure of the bitch at this time, and hope that once her desire has been achieved she will be satisfied. Unfortunately once a bitch has had a false pregnancy, it seems to be habit forming. With a sleek-bodied animal like an Italian Greyhound the outline can change dramatically. However, many bitches just have a slight swelling around the mammary gland area at this time, and if you try the above suggestions, it should disperse after about a month.

FRACTURES

Unfortunately these do occur in the legs of Italian Greyhounds. They are not delicate dogs, as described by some, but the fact is that they do have very long legs, and very fine bones, like those of a chicken, as can be seen by X-rays. Without either of these attributes the dog would not look like an Italian Greyhound! Their preference for leaping, running and jumping sometimes overcomes their sense of decorum, and a bad landing or misjudgement can cause an accident. In fact the result, while causing the dog to scream in pain – and it is a heart-rending noise – can soon be remedied in most instances, but it can distress the owner.

There seems to be no hereditary cause for this problem, and although explorations have been made as to whether diet, size, or exercise, play a part, no obvious connection has been made. However, I know some breeders who have definite views on whether to breed from stock where fractures have occurred too regularly. Fractures occur in both big and little dogs, and they mostly seem to happen during the adolescent period, which is generally when a puppy is at its silliest and has yet to learn the outcome of some of its actions. Obviously, there is no alternative but to seek veterinary help when a fracture occurs, but a few well tried and tested hints will not come amiss for the owner, in case of an emergency and to assist in the after-care.

If an accident occurs, this will usually be in a very simple manner, and you will be left to wonder why you did not prevent it happening. However, this will not undo what has happened, and no blame should be attached to the owner who has looked after their IG to the best of their ability and taken all necessary precautions against the possibility of a broken leg. It does remind us all that sensible rules concerning behaviour are necessary to allow humans and dogs to live alongside each other. If you have other pets, it is essential to pick up the injured dog and quickly and quietly shepherd the others into their beds. When a dog is injured, others will attack like a pack, and this applies to most breeds. It seems to release all the inherent instincts of the wild and causes obvious extra distress. Please do not think the worse of your other dogs if this happens; it is perfectly natural.

Steady the limb of the injured dog as much as possible. If you are capable of making some sort of splint to support it, well and good, but if you are alone, this is not easy, and most of us do not feel capable. Some experienced owners make very good use of various household articles like empty liquid soap bottles, syringes, etc., to make a support, but if you are not sure, then leave well alone. Try and remain calm; if necessary, sit for a few minutes with the IG. This will not add to its injury but will restore order in your own mind while you plan your actions. An injured IG may try and bite you in its pain. This is only a momentary forgetfulness; it has to blame somebody, and really it is trying to bite the hurt.

The owner should then contact the vet, and arrange to take the IG to the surgery as soon as possible. If possible, take someone with you to drive the car, so that you can hold the dog and reassure it. If this is not possible, place the dog in a small carrying container with plenty of soft bedding. Do not leave the dog loose in the vehicle, as more damage may result. When you arrive at the surgery, the vet will take charge.

It does no harm to ask if you may accompany the dog; most vets do not mind, if the owner is sufficiently calm, as it can help the Italian to know its owner is in the vicinity. It also does no harm to politely remind the vet, if he is not used to the breed, that IGs, like many hound breeds, do not respond well to anaesthetics and they can lose body heat very quickly. You must then have total confidence in your vet. There are so many different ways of repairing a fractured leg, and these are dependent on the skill of the vet and the type of break. The vet may simply plaster the leg, he may put special pins in it, or he may insert a plate. At any rate, you will have to trust his judgement. Always advise the vet of the last time the dog was fed, so he can calculate the anaesthetic.

The skill of the owner comes into play when the IG returns home. If the IG is still not conscious then it must be placed in a warm crate or cage, with a light blanket placed over the dog. It is advisable to turn the dog over every couple of hours, and it should not be left unattended until the anaesthetic has worn off completely. Initially you will feel clumsy about picking up your pet, but if you take care it should not be too uncomfortable. Talk quietly and encouragingly to the IG all the time, and make sure it is surrounded by soft bedding in its crate, so that if it tries to stand and wobbles over, it cannot damage itself by falling.

It is amazing just how fast IGs appear to feel fine again. Often on awaking their first thought is for their tummy, and they want some food straightaway. However, your vet will have advised you when you may offer a meal. The diet will have to be controlled to ensure no undue weight is carried on the leg. When the IG wishes to be clean it must be carried out and held carefully until you are sure it can stand unaided. It is a good idea to cut a plastic bag to size and cover the leg, so that urine does not wet the bandage; an old sock will suffice. This can then be removed when the dog returns inside. The owner must be very observant and notice if the bandage chafes the skin or if the foot should swell. Many do not think the whole foot should be encased in plaster or bandage, and certainly, strapping up is an art. If the foot swells, gently squeeze the toes to keep the circulation going, but if it is getting too distended then the vet must be advised.

An IG will often chew its bandage, and this is something also that must be watched. If there is a tendency, then place another lightweight bandage of your own, on top, and then this can be replaced as it gets torn. However, if the IG is really biting hard at the plaster and possibly feels hot to the touch, it is a sign that there could be a very sore place inside, and again the vet should be advised. Any unpleasant smell from the bandaging must also be reported immediately. Never be frightened to inform your vet of any problems, and you can always contact another IG owner or your Breed Club, where many experienced owners will be only too pleased to share practical help.

As the IG starts to mend it can be allowed out for gentle exercise in the garden – but be warned, if you have other dogs, as they will all assume it is back to normal. So exercise should be supervised at all times. However, make sure that the IG is not feeling left out of things because of the accident; it deserves a bit of spoiling. When the appointed time arrives for the covering to be removed the limb may look rather wasted, to the inexperienced eye. It does take time to recover the muscling. The callus on the bones may look unpleasant, but you would be surprised how quickly bones mend. Swimming, if it can be arranged, is very beneficial.

There have been several Italians who have gone on to become Champions after such an accident, so never think it is the end of the world. Some legs do not mend so well or so straight as others, but as long as the IG and the owner are happy, and there is no discomfort, then at least you have a healthy animal. Give it time and build up the exercise gradually. I hope this will not happen to your Italian, but at least if an owner feels these few tips will help, they will have served their purpose.

HOWLING TUMMY

This can sound awful, but it only means that there are a few gastric juices causing a disturbance. It can be caused by a change in diet, or the dog may have got hold of some rubbish. Try using something like milk of magnesia, in tablet or liquid form. This is very mild and often solves the problem. It will usually go away, left to its own devices, but be fairly uncomfortable for the little dog meanwhile, so it is worth attempting to ease the discomfort. Natural yoghurt is an easy and safe way of settling stomach upsets, particularly with puppies. Any sign of diarrhoea or blood in the faeces needs expert attention.

LAMENESS

This can be caused by a pulled muscle. Italians are running dogs and over-stretching or mistiming a landing can cause a pulled muscle. These can take a long time to cure, as only rest is the answer. Running cold water over the affected part may help. This works with horses, but there is a limit to how much of this treatment a little dog can tolerate. The only cure is patience – and when it is good and ready, nature will allow the dog to walk properly. In the first instance, it is worth checking feet to be sure there are no cuts to pads or foreign bodies that could be causing the problem. If you spot anything wrong, remove the thorn or grit or whatever, and then soak the foot in salt water. On hot days melted tar or hot pavements can burn the pads.

If the lameness is caused by Patella Luxation, this will be noticed on a regular basis. It can be seen as a skipping action on one of the back legs while the dog is the move. The knee cap will also straighten out because the groove is too shallow for the patella. This condition is not common in Italians, although it does occur in a number of small toy breeds. A dog can also damage this joint by knocking the leg against a high step or by falling, and veterinary advice must be sought.

MASTITIS

This is caused by inflammation of the mammary area, in the nursing mother. This is a serious condition and should be attended to immediately by your vet.

METRITIS AND PYOMETRA

These are diseases of the womb, and the bitch must receive medical attention. The signs vary from bitch to bitch, but in simple terms, a very severe discharge may be observed or a season may seem not to cease at the appropriate time. Bleeding in-between seasons is not usual, and advice is needed. The bitch's temperature may also fluctuate. The bitch will generally have various symptoms that her caring owner should immediately notice, and the vet will advise.

However, my most recent experience of pyometra was in a Whippet bitch, and there was no discharge other than a mere speck on a couple of occasions. Surgery showed that her womb was about three times its normal size, and yet this not detected by external examination. Sometimes a bitch suffering from pyometra will have to be spayed, i.e. the uterus will have to be removed. Many breeders prefer to have their older bitches spayed in any event. It usually precludes the onset of any growths in later life, and, of course, it means no more seasons for the bitch.

NAILS

Nails must be kept trimmed back. Black nails are more difficult to cut because it is impossible to see the quick, but the lighter ones are easy. The quick is the sensitive nerve that is in the centre of the nail, and it can be seen in the lighter coloured dogs as a pink line. The nail should be cut below where this finishes. Cutting the quick will make the nail bleed, and it is wise to have one of the proprietary powders available to dab on to stop the bleeding as quickly as possible. No harm will come to the dog if it bleeds for a few minutes, so do not panic. Many dogs hate the procedure, so firm handling is required. Some owners find it easier if someone holds the dog while they cut the nails.

PANCREAS DISORDERS

These do occur occasionally, and the dog will not seem to gain weight at all. This is not to be confused with youngsters who do not seem to put on sufficient weight to please their owners, which usually happens just when they are ready for the show ring! Bearing in mind the active nature of the Italian, they do run off a lot of fat in everyday living. It is also important to study the family of dogs they have been bred from, as weight variations may be a family trait. In severe pancreas disorders the dog may lose white faeces, and it may be drinking excessively. Sometimes a dog will eat a great deal of food but not put on any weight gain. The owner must be aware of the problem, and then seek advice.

PERTHES DISEASE

There have been one or two cases over the years of this disease, which is usually associated with young children. The owner will notice the obvious deformity of the hip region and medical advice will be necessary.

TAILS

These can be damaged by banging or shaking against a hard surface. The bones in the tail are so small, like a series of small pieces of china, and these can break if they are knocked with sufficient force. Sometimes puppies are born with a definite kink in the tail, or clumsy mothers can break a tail when nursing. A kink cannot be remedied, and a break also causes problems. It sometimes helps to repeatedly run your fingers down the tail to push the bones in place – it does not seem to bother the dogs. I do not recommend placing the tail in plaster, as I have known dogs to lose the piece of the tail that has been covered.

TEETH

Italian Greyhounds do seem to have problems with their teeth, and so they must be looked after throughout a dog's life. Regular cleaning is a must. Funnily enough, it is not necessarily the bigger specimens that have the best teeth; I have known some very small dogs to have a lovely set of teeth and others to lose them early. I feel some families of dogs have better teeth than others. Some of the smaller specimens may have jumbled teeth and some can be misaligned.

Occasionally, in young puppies, the 'baby' canines will not come out naturally and may seem to be pushing the second set of canines out of alignment. If this is the case your vet will usually advise the removal of the baby set to allow free growth. If they are not causing any problems, but are a nuisance because they will not drop out, you may be able to loosen the teeth by gently wiggling them with your thumb while the puppy is on your lap. Rough games of tug-of-war with a piece of towelling also help to loosen them. In cases of severe misalignment you will need to be guided by your vet. Any corrective treatment may be very uncomfortable for the IG. As long as the dog is happy and comfortable it is usually better to leave any untidy teeth, but again, your vet will advise. Exhibition may be prohibited because dentition is assessed by the judges in the ring, but there are more things in the life of an IG than the show ring.

Some vets will prescribe a mild sedative for use at home, so that you can give your dog's teeth a thorough cleaning without any stress on the dog. However, care must be taken as 'fitting' has been associated with some types of medication. I recommend wiping the gums over with a sterilising solution, such as the type used for cleaning babies' bottles, and this will leave the gums healthy and clean. If the dog is still and quiet, all the offending material and tartar can be removed. Loose threads of food matter can accumulate round the teeth, and this can result in foul breath and eventually abscesses in the gums. The unpleasant substances will penetrate the whole system of the dog, and this can make their old age very uncomfortable. Incidentally, abscesses on the cheek under the eye are usually caused by infection in the tooth or gum; diseases of the gums often cause more distress to older dogs than any other condition. In severe cases your vet will advise that the dog should have some teeth removed, and then he should give the remaining teeth a thorough cleaning while the dog is anaesthetised at the surgery.

VACCINATION
Vaccination against the various infectious diseases is essential, and you must be guided by your medical adviser as to inoculation or homoeopathic methods, as favoured by many people today.

WORMING
This is essential for all puppies, and both conventional and homoeopathic treatments are available. It is equally important for adults to be kept free of worms, and a bitch should always be wormed before mating. The simple dosing can be done approximately twice a year to ensure full protection; those that need to protect against heartworm and other parasites should be advised by their own practitioner.

CARE OF THE VETERAN ITALIAN GREYHOUND
Italian Greyhounds often reach a fine old age, and dogs aged between fifteen and twenty years have been recorded, although the latter is rare. It also a well known fact that the male's ability to sire stock is not always impaired by the onset of old age, although if you are intending to use a very old dog at stud the possibility of infertility does have to be considered. Older bitches should not be expected to rear puppies, even though I have known accidental matings of bitches aged ten years to be successful, but it is not to be recommended. I think that eight years of age should be the upper limit for assuming maternal duties, and then only if she has already had a litter – she should never have a litter at this age for the first time.

In general, Italians are no different from other breeds as regards health care in old age; some 'wear better' than others. Unfortunately, many solid coloured IGs tend to look grey around the muzzle from about two years of age onwards, for some reason that I cannot explain. Coats also vary, and if a dog suffers from baldness this certainly detracts from its appearance. The reds and whites definitely score on this point; they seem to be less prone to the condition, and dogs living in sunnier climates also have an advantage.

Mammary tumours are as common in IGs as in any other breed, and sometimes other growths may appear. These will have to be treated by your vet. In my own opinion, it is better to neuter bitches in middle age, to prevent any troubles of the uterus developing. If the operation is performed when the bitch is in good health, and in the middle of seasons, there should be no complications and she will recover in a couple of days. As soon as the stitches have been removed, if not before, the bitch will be back to normal, but without the potential problems caused by coming into season. Some lumps are certainly best left untreated, unless they become a bother to the little dog, as surgery to remove them can make their reappearance more speedy. Your vet will advise the best course of action.

Stiffness of the joints can develop, particularly in the hindquarters, and care should be taken to ensure that your Italian does not get wet or cold, and always has a soft, warm bed to lie in. Always make sure your IG is well and truly dry after bathing, and does not become chilled. Outdoor coats must be thoroughly waterproof; if not, they must be removed as quickly as possible after exercise and never allowed to dry on the dog. Sometimes a dog that has suffered a fracture in the front legs may be prone to arthritic pain, and it may appear a little lame. There may also be a tendency for a dog to get slacker on the pasterns over old injuries.

Exercise should not be forced on any elderly Italians; some are quite happy to go on long hikes, others will be quite happy to have a gambol in their own house and garden, if they are allowed free range. An enforced long walk along pavements may promote good muscle toning in a youngster, but it will not be appreciated by an older IG. The elderly dog will tend to sleep a lot more, only getting up when something exciting is happening in the household.

The neck can sometimes be a source of discomfort in the hound type of breeds. Persistent dampness or a sudden twist or turn at any age can cause a dislocation, as it can in humans. An IG's elegant, long neck can be quite vulnerable, and any reluctance to eat from the food dish, with a preference to curl up in a bed should be investigated. Many dogs benefit from having their food bowl raised on a small stool, or similar. Chiropracters have been known to help with some disorders.

Poor eyesight, and sometimes eventual blindness, is as common in elderly Italians as in people. Nothing can be done except for avoiding any changes of furniture in the area that the dog is used to. Many live for many years quite happily, and while they are still enjoying their life and food, they need no different treatment. Obviously care must be taken that the dog is not annoyed by youngsters, but I found that when I had a blind, elderly IG, she knew when to keep to her own bed when there was too much excitement, and only put in an appearance when the coast was clear!

Diet should be controlled; a fat dog is not a healthy dog, at any age. If, on the other hand, the dog loses weight and is eating well, there may be a medical reason, and the vet should be informed. The problem could be caused by liver or kidney disease. Owners should always observe their dogs carefully, and any change in faeces or excessive drinking or urinating should be noted, as all factors may have relevance to a vet.

Teeth can cause problems in Italian Greyhounds, and it is doubly important not to neglect this part of their hygiene as your dog gets older. As the teeth loosen with age, food particles get trapped and gums recede, and the breath will smell foul. With the sort of breed who likes a lot of attention, this can be very offensive to their owners. Neglect will allow abscesses to form and gum disease, which in turn will soon cause poisons to enter the system of the dog and result in a very fast deterioration in their general well-being. Most dogs dislike having their teeth cleaned, but it is time well spent. If a dog has loose teeth and a toothbrush is considered too harsh, then a piece of lint or towel, dipped into some suitable cleaning agent, will be kinder. If necessary, teeth will have to be removed, and the cleaning done by the vet. However, nobody wishes to inflict anaesthesia too often on an Italian Greyhound, particularly an elderly dog, and therefore regular inspection and cleaning by the owner will help. There are several proprietary materials available these days specifically manufactured for dogs, and the instructions should be followed carefully.

It is amazing how fast nails grow when dogs are not being exercised regularly, and so these must be kept trimmed. The longer they are left the more difficult it is to cut them nice and short. The quick also seems to grow. IGs spending hours under their blankets or on their owner's bed will not be wearing them down naturally and if they should become entangled in any woollen material or similar, it is comparatively easy for a nail to be pulled out and the quick exposed. Of course, a nail can be damaged, or ripped at any age, and if this should occur a novice owner will find the consequent bleeding quite upsetting, as they do seem to bleed a lot. However, it is not as bad as it may first appear. If a nail should be 'hanging on by a thread' as it were, then you must either get veterinary attention or have the courage to cut it off. Fast, bold action is better than fussing around and causing the dog more distress. Powder to quell the bleeding is available.

In a household where several IGs are kept, never allow yourself to to forget your older IG. It is so easy to become involved with the newest puppy, with the training, and outings to shows. However, the older IG will still want time with the owner; time to sneak into bed for five minutes, time to cuddle up in a chair and push its head up to the owner's face; time to be loved and cared for. We all know that time is the one thing that everyone is short of, but it is the biggest gift you can give to your old Italian Greyhound.

While IGs can live to a great age, this is not always the case, and an accident could happen or an illness could develop, causing a great deal of distress to the dog and owner alike. Veterinary skills are extremely advanced these days, if sometimes somewhat expensive, and therefore insurance schemes are well worth considering when you first purchase a dog of any breed. As long as an old dog is happy and content, and has a fine quality of life, then its life should be preserved as a precious commodity. When this is no longer the case, no matter how distressing it is for the owner to face the prospect of separation, the option of euthanasia must be considered. If you have formed a good relationship with your vet, then when the time comes, your little dog will be given a dignified end to any suffering by a simple injection. You will usually be allowed to hold the patient in your arms, and I always do this, talking and comforting all the while, as life slips away. This is always a very sad experience, whether the dog is five or fifteen years old.

Over the years I have attended the same surgery, and I am not ashamed to say that my vet has witnessed me tearfully executing this last duty on a number of occasions. It is certainly not easy, whether you own one or several dogs, but this is the last act of kindness you can bestow to ensure that dignity is retained to the last. You, the owner, will have to face the loss of companionship, but at least you can prevent your dog suffering more than is necessary. We must not be selfish at the end, and hanging on to life at all costs is no way to reward a faithful friend, who has served us so well over the years.